SIDE BY SIDE

Spanish & English

GRAMMAR

Third Edition

Edith R. Farrell and C. Frederick Farrell Jr., PhD

Mc Graw Hill

New York   Chicago   San Francisco   Lisbon   London   Madrid   Mexico City
Milan   New Delhi   San Juan   Seoul   Singapore   Sydney   Toronto

To our parents and first teachers

1 2 3 4 5 6 7 8 9 10 11 12 13 14 15 16 17   QDB/QDB   1 9 8 7 6 5 4 3 2

ISBN   978-0-07-178861-8
MHID   0-07-178861-1

e-ISBN 978-0-07-178862-5
e-MHID 0-07-178862-X

Library of Congress Control Number 2011937085

Interior design by Village Bookworks

Contents

Preface v

Introduction vii

1 Introducing languages

A short history of English 2
A short history of Spanish 3

2 Parts of speech

Introducing the parts of speech 6

3 Nouns

Introducing nouns 10
Introducing subjects and objects 14
Introducing determiners 16

4 Pronouns

Introducing pronouns 20
Personal pronouns 22
Possessive pronouns 28
Reflexive/reciprocal pronouns 30
Disjunctive pronouns 32
Relative pronouns 34
How to analyze relative pronouns 36
Demonstrative pronouns 38
Interrogative pronouns 40

5 Adjectives

Introducing adjectives 44
Descriptive adjectives 46
Comparison of adjectives 48
Proper adjectives 50
Limiting adjectives 50
Demonstrative adjectives 50
Possessive adjectives 52
Interrogative adjectives 54
Indefinite adjectives 54
Other limiting adjectives 56
Other adjectival forms 56

6 Adverbs

Introducing adverbs 60

7 Conjunctions

Introducing conjunctions 66

8 Interjections

Introducing interjections 70

9 Prepositions

Introducing prepositions 74

10 Verbs

Introducing verbs 80
Introducing questions 82
Introducing verbals 84
Present infinitives 84
Past infinitives 84
Gerunds 86
Participles 86
Indicative mood 90
Present tenses 90
Past tenses 94
Imperfect tense 95
Preterite tense 97
Future tenses 98
Conditional tenses 100
Perfect tenses 102
Present perfect tense 102
Present perfect progressive tense 104
Past perfect (pluperfect) tense 104
Past perfect progressive tense 106
Preterite perfect tense 107
Future perfect tense 108
Future perfect progressive tense 108
Conditional perfect tense 110
Conditional perfect progressive tense 110
Passive voice 112
Imperative mood 114
Subjunctive mood 116
Imperfect subjunctive 121
Present perfect subjunctive 122
Past perfect (pluperfect) subjunctive 123

Exercises 125

Appendices

A Comparison of interrogative pronouns and interrogative adjectives 172
B *Para* and *por* 173
C Uses of *ser* and *estar* 175

Answer key 177

Preface

Side by Side Spanish & English Grammar presents the essential elements of Spanish grammar—usually covered in a high school program or in the first year of college Spanish—"side by side" with their English counterparts. This comparative/contrastive approach allows students to build on what they already know, as they see the ways in which English and Spanish are similar, and to avoid potential trouble spots.

Side by Side Spanish & English Grammar has been used in both high school and college Spanish classes, and even in some English classes for a few students who were having trouble in understanding their English grammar text. Its vocabulary is, for the most part, limited to the most frequently used Spanish words.

It has been used as

1. a reference book for beginning students, for whom the standard works are too complex to be useful. This allows students a means for independent inquiry.

2. a means of quick review of material forgotten over the summer or material missed because of illness.

3. a means of helping a student in a new school catch up with the class.

4. a means of organizing or summarizing material presented in the primary text, especially for students whose learning style favors an "organized approach."

5. a means of providing a common background for talking about language with students who have studied English in different ways, so that their study of Spanish will show them something about how language works, one of the expectations of many college language requirements.

6. an alternative method of explaining grammatical points in both English and Spanish to relieve the classroom teacher of the task.

Special features of the book that students will find useful include

1. a standard format that introduces each part of speech and answers the most common questions about it.

2. Quick Check charts that allow students to express themselves with more confidence, since they can independently check their sentences against a model.

3. appendices that identify and summarize trouble spots, such as the differences between interrogative pronouns and adjectives, and the uses of *ser* and *estar, por* and *para*.

4. an exercise section that tests understanding of the main grammatical areas covered in the book, plus Using your Spanish, a section new to this edition, that prepares students for communication in Spanish.

We hope that this text will provide ways for students to increase their independent work and to adapt material to their own learning styles and situations.

Acknowledgments

I remain thankful, as I know my late wife, Edith R. Farrell, would, to our colleague, formerly at the University of Minnesota, Morris: Dr. Stacy Parker Aronson, who read the manuscript of this book; and David Stillman, who compiled the exercise section.

Preliminary studies on which *Side by Side French & English Grammar,* the companion volume of this book, was based were supported in part by a grant from the Educational Development Program of the University of Minnesota.

Introduction

This book grew out of a series of supplements to a Spanish grammar text. Its purpose is to help you learn Spanish more easily.

Many students have had trouble with foreign languages because they have not looked carefully enough, or critically enough, at their own. Struggles with your own language took place at such an early age that you have forgotten the times when it seemed difficult. Now it seems perfectly natural to you, and it is hard to adapt to different ways of expressing ideas.

The material in this book has been classified and arranged to show you English and your new language "side by side." You may be surprised at how many grammatical elements are similar in the two languages.

Information that is the same for both English and Spanish is usually not repeated on facing pages. If you find that a section is omitted under the Spanish, look to your left and find it on the English page. The English meaning of a Spanish example is usually on the left-hand page, too.

Why grammar?

People can speak, read, or write their native language, at least to a reasonable degree, without studying formal grammar (the rules governing how we say, change, and arrange words to express our ideas). Just by being around other speakers, we hear millions of examples, and the patterns we hear become a part of us. Even babies start with correct basic patterns (subject-verb-object), even though words may be missing or incorrect: "Me wants cookie!"

Knowledge of grammar helps a great deal, though, in testing new and more complex words or patterns and in analyzing one's writing to discover where a sentence went wrong or how it could be more effective. Sometimes, "It sounds right (or wrong)" won't help.

All of the explanations in this book reflect standard English or Spanish. You may sometimes think, "I don't say that!" The important word here is "say." We often ignore some rules in conversation, or even in informal writing such as friendly letters. When you are writing an important paper or giving a speech, however, you may want to use the standard form in order to make the best possible impression. You will also find that knowing grammar will help you in your study of language.

In learning a foreign language, grammar is necessary because it tells you how to choose the right word—or the right form of a word that you are using for the first time. It is not the way that you acquired your native language as a child, but it is an efficient way for adults who want to express more complex ideas and do not want to make any more mistakes than absolutely necessary.

Grammar saves you time and prevents many mistakes by guiding you in your choices.

1

Introducing languages

A short history of English

What we now know as England was settled in the fifth and sixth centuries A.D. by Germanic tribes like the Angles, the Saxons, and the Jutes—all speaking related, but distinct, dialects. Later, in the ninth century, Scandinavian invaders came, bringing their languages, which also contributed to English. Political power determined the centers of learning, which contained the literature of continental Europe, written in Latin, as well as contributions of the inhabitants of Britain. By the ninth century, the primary center was in Wessex, due to the Viking invasions in the north, and so the West Saxon dialect became standard as Old English. It was heavily inflected, with endings on nouns to show many cases and on verbs to show time and person.

This was the language current in 1066, when William the Conqueror, from the province of Normandy in what is now France, won the battle of Hastings and became ruler of England. The natives knew no French; William and his followers did not speak Old English. For a long time, each group continued to speak its own language, but gradually they merged. Since the governing group spoke French, we often find that words for work, home, and ordinary things come from Old English, while words for leisure or artistic goods come from French.

Wamba, the jester in Sir Walter Scott's *Ivanhoe,* made a joke about this, saying that cows and pigs were Anglo-Saxon while the peasants took care of them, but became French (beef and pork) when they were ready to be eaten. In the same way, "house" looks and sounds like the German word *Haus,* but "mansion" looks like the French word for "house," *maison.*

English often uses several words with a similar meaning, with the more elegant word frequently being of French origin. For example, instead of "give," we may say "donate," which is like the French *donner*; instead of "mean," we may say "signify," from French *signifier.*

Latin, the language of the church and therefore of learning in general throughout all Europe, also had an influence on English. Around 1500, English absorbed about 25 percent of known Latin vocabulary. English, therefore, is basically a Germanic language, but one to which large portions of French and Latin were added.

Latin gave rise to both French and Spanish, and it continued to influence both languages for many centuries. Therefore, some English words with French or Latin roots have Spanish cognates. Compare the following.

GERMANIC ROOT (COMMON)	FRENCH ROOT (ELEGANT)	LATIN ROOT (LEARNED)	SPANISH COGNATE
ask	*question*	*interrogate*	*interrogar*
goodness	*virtue*	*probity*	*virtud*
better	*improve*	*ameliorate*	—
rider	*cavalier*	*equestrian*	*caballero*

Today English is recognized as an international language and has a significant impact on other cultures. The proximity of Latin America to the United States and the growing number of Hispanics in this country have also given an increasingly important place to the Spanish language here. A number of Spanish words have come into everyday use in the United States, for example, *tango, taco, hacienda,* and *barrio.* Their meaning in everyday English contexts, however, may be more limited or even entirely different from the original Spanish meaning.

A short history of Spanish

Spanish is one of the Romance languages, like French, Italian, and others, that have developed from Latin. Although there are differences in vocabulary and pronunciation of Spanish as it is spoken in Spain, Latin America, and other parts of the world, what we call Spanish is essentially derived from Castilian, the dialect of the historic Spanish region of Castile. As a result, many Spanish speakers refer to the Spanish language as *el castellano.*

When the Romans invaded the Iberian Peninsula in the second and first centuries B.C., they encountered different peoples with different languages. When these peoples learned Latin from the Roman soldiers, they pronounced the words a little differently, because they continued to use the familiar sounds of their own languages. They retained other important elements of their original languages, especially vocabulary. Other peoples, like those in northern Italy and Gaul (now France), did the same thing.

This continued until the "Latin" of different countries evolved into different, though related, languages. Now, while you can guess at words and even forms and rules in a Romance language, based on your knowledge of one of them, a speaker of Spanish cannot be understood by a speaker of French, and vice versa. As in English, Latin words were added to Spanish in the sixteenth century to form a "learned" language.

After the time of the Romans, the Visigoths and other Germanic tribes entered the Peninsula. They were followed by the Arabic-speaking Moors, who invaded Spain in 711 and inhabited most of it until the Reconquest of Spain was complete in 1492, when the Catholic monarchs Ferdinand and Isabella reclaimed the land. In that same year, Jews and Muslims were expelled from Spanish soil, and Columbus arrived in what would become the Americas. The Moors left a lasting influence on many aspects of Spanish culture, including its architecture, music, and dance; the influence of Arabic on the Spanish language can be seen in words such as *algebra, alfombra,* and *ojalá.*

The sound system of Spanish continued to evolve in significant ways. Italianisms were introduced during the Renaissance, as they were throughout much of Europe. Spain was strongly influenced by the French monarchy in the eighteenth century, resulting in overly refined speech that mimicked French. As the Industrial Revolution took hold in the nineteenth century, Spanish vocabulary adapted to accommodate the changing world.

All languages change, and the trend is toward less inflection. Distinctions that seem to be too hard or unnecessary die out. Over the centuries, different languages have eliminated different linguistic elements. For example, in Latin and other older languages, every noun had gender, number, and case (which indicated its function in a sentence). In fact, modern German still uses all three grammatical distinctions.

In English, we pay little attention to grammatical gender, but nouns still have number (singular and plural) and an additional case (the possessive), while pronouns also have an objective case; the functions of other cases are expressed by word order and prepositions. Spanish has no cases for nouns referring to things, but when referring to persons, the subject is distinguished from the object not only by word order but also by the preposition *a*, which normally precedes the object noun. Spanish has grammatical gender and number for all nouns. You will notice other instances in which Spanish and English differ. Comparing languages is interesting, because it points out the important elements in each language. Let's examine the forms of a common masculine noun in Germanic languages.

| | MODERN GERMAN | | OLD ENGLISH | | MODERN ENGLISH |
	SINGULAR	PLURAL	SINGULAR	PLURAL	SINGULAR/PLURAL
SUBJECT	*der König*	*die Könige*	*se cyning*	*tha cyningas*	*the king/kings*
GENITIVE	*des Königs*	*der Könige*	*thoes cyning*	*thara cyninga*	*the king's/kings'*
DATIVE	*dem König*	*den Königen*	*thaem cyninge*	*thaem cyningum*	*to the king/kings*
OBJECTIVE	*den König*	*die Könige*	*thone cyning*	*tha cyningas*	*the king/kings*

Declension (listing all the case forms of a noun) in German is further complicated by having feminine and neuter nouns whose definite articles and endings are different from the example above, as well as irregular nouns, which have different forms altogether. Adjectives in modern German also have different endings for each gender and case.

Now, let's compare Latin, Spanish, and English forms in the present-tense conjugation of the verb "to have."

LATIN		MODERN SPANISH		MODERN ENGLISH	
habeo	*habemus*	*he*	*hemos*	*I have*	*we have*
habes	*habetis*	*has*	*habéis*	*you have*	*you have*
habet	*habent*	*ha*	*han*	*he has*	*they have*

The endings in Latin and Spanish are so distinctive that it is not necessary to indicate the subject. The *h* is often not pronounced in many European languages, and never in standard Spanish. *V* and *b* are very similar sounds, and in Spanish they are almost identical. Modern English is the least inflected of the modern languages referenced here, French is next, then Italian, Spanish, and German.

Introducing the parts of speech

2

Parts of speech

Introducing the parts of speech

Both English and Spanish words are categorized by parts of speech. You may have learned these in elementary school without understanding their usefulness. They are important, because different rules apply to the different categories. In your own language, you do this naturally, unless the word is new to you. You know to say *one horse, two horses*, adding an *-s* to make the noun *horse* plural. You do not try to apply a noun's rule to a verb and say *I am, we ams*; instead, you say *we are*. People learning a foreign language sometimes use the wrong set of rules, however, because all of the forms are new, so nothing "sounds wrong." To avoid this kind of mistake, learn the part of speech when you learn a new vocabulary word.

Parts of speech help you identify words, so that even if a word is used in several ways (and this happens in both English and Spanish), you can determine the Spanish equivalent. For instance, *that* can be

1. a conjunction.

    I know **that** Mary is coming.
    *Yo sé **que** María viene.*

2. a demonstrative adjective.

    That person is impossible.
    ***Esa** persona es imposible.*

3. a pronoun.

    I didn't know **that**.
    *Yo no sabía **eso**.*

When you know the parts of speech, the fact that a word is used several ways in English won't cause you to choose the wrong one in Spanish.

Following is a list of the parts of speech. The parts are described (1) in traditional definitions, (2) by the forms that identify them, and (3) by their functions (as structural linguists think of them).

Nouns

1. Names or words standing for persons, places, things, or abstract concepts

    John
    man
    Madrid
    city
    table
    justice

2. Words that become plural by adding *-s* or *-es* (in addition to a few other ways)

    book ~ books
    fox ~ foxes
    child ~ children

3. Words that function as subjects, objects, or complements

    ***John** is here.*
    *She read the **book**.*
    *There is **Mary**.*

Pronouns

1. Words that substitute for nouns

    *John is already here. Have you seen **him**?*

2. Words that are used when no noun is identified

    ***It** is raining.*
    ***They** say . . .*
    ***You** never know.*

3. Words that serve the same function as nouns

    ***He** is here.*
    ***He** loves **her**.*
    *There **it** is.*

Adjectives

1. Words that modify, limit, or qualify a noun or pronoun

    dumb
    red
    serious
    happy

2. Words that may be inflected (may change form) or may be preceded by *more* or *most* to make comparisons

    dumb ~ *dumber* ~ *dumbest*
    serious ~ **more** *serious* ~ **most** *serious*

Verbs

1. Words that express action, existence, or state of being

    speak
    learn
    run
    be
    have
    feel

2. Words that may be inflected to show person (*I **am** ~ he **is***), time (*I **sing** ~ I **sang***), voice (*I **write** ~ it **is written***), and mood (*if I **am** here ~ if I **were** you*)

Adverbs

1. Words that modify verbs, adjectives, or other adverbs by telling how, when, where, or how much

    *We'll come **soon**.*
    *It's **really** big.*
    *They do it **very** well.*

2. Words that can show comparison between verbs (as adjectives do for nouns)

    soon ~ *soon**er*** ~ *soon**est***
    rapidly ~ **more** *rapidly* ~ **most** *rapidly*

Prepositions

1. Words that express place, time, and other circumstances and show the relationship between two elements in a sentence

    at
    for
    in
    of
    on
    to

2. Words that are not inflected (never change form)

3. Words that have a noun or pronoun as their object

    in *a minute*
    of *a sort*
    on *it*

These groups are called prepositional phrases.

Conjunctions

1. Coordinating conjunctions (for example, *and*, *but*, and *so*) connect words, phrases, or clauses that are grammatically equivalent.

    *John **and** Mary*
    *on the table, **but** under a napkin*
    *I had no money, **so** I stayed at home.*

2. Subordinating conjunctions (for example, *if*, *because*, and *when*) connect subordinate clauses to the main clause of a sentence.

    ***When** you see it, you will believe me.*

Interjections

1. Exclamations

    Hey!
    Wow!

2. Words that can be used alone or in sentences

    Darn!
    ***Oh**, Mary, is it true?*

3

Nouns

English Introducing nouns

Definition See page 6.

Forms English nouns are considered to have gender, number, and case.

GENDER Masculine or feminine gender is used only for someone or something that is male or female.

> *man*
> *woman*
> *bull*
> *tigress*

All other nouns are neuter. Gender makes no difference in English except when there are two forms for one noun (for example, *actor* and *actress*) or when the nouns are replaced by pronouns (for example, *he, she, it*).

NUMBER Most nouns add *-s* or *-es* to the singular form to form the plural.

> *train ~ trains*
> *box ~ boxes*

Some nouns have irregular plural forms.

> *mouse ~ mice*
> *man ~ men*
> *child ~ children*

CASE There is only one extra case in English: the possessive, or genitive. It is formed by adding *-'s* to a singular noun or *-'* to a plural noun ending in *-s*.

> **Mary's** *book*
> *the* **book's** *cover*
> *the* **books'** *covers*

The possessive case can often be ignored, and *of* used instead, although this form is less common when a person is involved.

> *Kant's theories → the theories* ***of Kant***
> *the book's pages → the pages* ***of the book***

Nouns are often preceded by determiners (see page 16).

> ***a*** *book,* **the** *book,* **my** *book,* **two** *books*

Uses The three most common uses of nouns are as subjects, objects, and complements (see page 14).

SUBJECT	**Mrs. Gómez** *is Spanish.*
APPOSITIVE	*Mrs. Gómez, a Spanish* **woman***, is visiting us.*
DIRECT OBJECT OF A VERB	*He has a* **pencil***.*
INDIRECT OBJECT OF A VERB	*She gave the hat to* **John***.*
OBJECT OF A PREPOSITION	*We are in the* **room***.*
COMPLEMENT	*It is a valuable* **book***.*
ADJECTIVE	*I have my* **history** *textbook.*

CONTINUED ON PAGE 12 ►

Definition   See page 6.

Forms   Spanish nouns are considered to have gender and number, but not case.

GENDER   All nouns in Spanish are either masculine or feminine; there are no neuter nouns. When you learn a Spanish noun, you must also learn whether it is masculine or feminine.

The gender of nouns is very important in Spanish, since their determiners and the adjectives accompanying them must be of the same gender. If a noun is preceded by *el,* it is almost always masculine; *la* designates a feminine noun. For pronunciation reasons, there is an exception for feminine nouns that begin with a stressed *a,* and *el* is used before these nouns. For example, we say **el** *agua,* even though *agua* is a feminine noun.

NUMBER   Spanish nouns that end in a vowel add -*s* to form the plural; nouns that end in a consonant add -*es* to form the plural. A plural noun also has a plural article. *Los* is the plural article for masculine nouns, and *las* is the plural feminine article.

> el centavo ~ los centavos
> la casa ~ las casas
> el color ~ los colores
> la ciudad ~ las ciudades

Family names do not have a regular plural form. If they end in -*s* or -*z,* the name remains unchanged. However, if a family name ends in an unaccented vowel, it is sometimes made plural, but usually not.

> los Rodríguez
> los Castro OR los Castros

CASE   Spanish nouns do not have different cases. Possession is indicated by the preposition *de,* plus an article if one is needed.

> las teorías **de** Kant
> las páginas **del** libro

Spanish nouns are often preceded by determiners (see pages 17–18).

> **un** libro, **el** libro, **mi** libro, **dos** libros

Uses   Nouns are used in the same way in Spanish and English. Compare the following sentences with the English sentences on the opposite page.

> **La señora Gómez** es española.
> La señora Gómez, una **mujer** española, nos visita.
> Él tiene un **lápiz**.
> Ella le dio el sombrero a **Juan**.
> Estamos en el **cuarto**.
> Es un **libro** valioso.
> Tengo mi texto **de historia**.

Rarely is a Spanish noun used alone as an adjective; a phrase, usually with *de,* is used.

CONTINUED ON PAGE 13 ▶

Types There are several ways to classify nouns. Following are two important ones.

1. Common vs. proper

   Common nouns are applied to a class of individuals. They begin with a lowercase letter.

   student
   country
   cat
   language

   Proper nouns name a specific individual within a class. They begin with a capital letter.

   Miss Jones
   Mexico
   Kitty
   English

2. Countable vs. mass

   Countable nouns can be counted.

   one pencil
   two sharks
   three engineers

   Mass nouns cannot be separated into individuals—they cannot be counted.

   salt
   weather
   sadness

Spanish Introducing nouns (continued)

Types   Spanish nouns may be classified as follows.

1. Common vs. proper

   For the most part, Spanish is the same as English in this classification, but there are a few important differences. Nouns for languages, days of the week, and months are common nouns in Spanish and do not require a capital letter.

English	*el inglés*
Monday	*lunes*
October	*octubre*

2. Countable vs. mass

   This classification follows the same principle in Spanish as in English. However, mass nouns such as *la gente* and *el pueblo* are always treated as singular.

Introducing subjects and objects

Subjects

Subjects are most frequently nouns or pronouns. The subject of a verb is the person or thing that *is* something or *is doing* something.

> **Mary** and **I** *are here.*
> **John** *speaks Spanish.*
> *Are* **they** (the textbooks) *arriving today?*

✓ QUICK CHECK

Ask yourself: *Who* is here? *Who* speaks Spanish? *What* is arriving?

Answer: the subject

In normal word order, the subject comes before the verb. The subject is often, but not always, the first word in a sentence or clause.

Subject complements

Subject complements are words or phrases that define, or complete an idea about, the subject.

> *Mr. White is a* **professor**.
> *Jeanne and Alice are* **Americans**.

Direct objects

Some systems of grammar refer to direct objects as "object complements." The name matters less than the ability to recognize their important function. Direct objects are usually nouns or pronouns that directly receive the verb's action. In normal word order, the direct object comes after the verb.

> *Mary likes* **John**. *She likes* **him**.
> *The professor is giving a* **test**. *He is giving* **it**.

✓ QUICK CHECK

Ask yourself: *Who* is liked? *What* is being given?

Answer: the direct object

Indirect objects

Indirect objects are usually nouns or pronouns that are indirectly affected by the verb's action. They indicate *to* whom or *for* whom something is done.

> *Speak* **to me**!

Verbs of communication often have implied direct objects, as in *Tell me (the news)*. These objects are sometimes expressed in other languages.

COMBINATIONS Some verbs (for example, *give*, *tell*, and *buy*) can have more than one object. In addition to a direct object, there can be an indirect object. Counting the subject, there can be three nouns or pronouns with different functions, even in a short sentence.

> **Robert** *gives* **the book** **to Alice**.
> SUBJECT   DIRECT OBJECT   INDIRECT OBJECT
>
> **Robert** *gives* **Alice** **the book**.
> SUBJECT   INDIRECT OBJECT DIRECT OBJECT
>
> **He** *gives* **it** **to her**.
> SUBJECT   DIRECT OBJECT INDIRECT OBJECT

Notice that the two possible word orders have no effect on which object is direct and which is indirect. The word order in English simply determines whether or not the word *to* is used.

✓ QUICK CHECK

To analyze the sentences above, ask yourself: *Who gives?*

Answer: *Robert* or *he* (the subject)

Who or *what* is given?

Answer: *the book* or *it* (the direct object)

To/for whom / to/for what is it given?

Answer: *Alice* or *her* (the indirect object)

Objects of prepositions

Every preposition must have an object (see page 7). This object immediately follows the preposition.

> on the **table** ~ on **it**
> after **Peter** ~ after **him**

In questions and relative clauses in English (see page 74), this rule is often ignored, and the preposition is used alone at the end of the sentence.

> **To whom** did you give it?
> → **Whom** did you give it **to**?

The first sentence is considered standard English. Spanish uses the same patterns as standard English.

Spanish reverse construction verbs

With Spanish reverse construction verbs that take an indirect object pronoun, the verb agrees with the subject, not the indirect object (which may be the subject in English). Consider these examples with *gustar* ("to be pleasing to," "to like").

> Me **gustan las tortillas**.
> I like tortillas.
>
> A las chicas les **gusta el chocolate**.
> The girls like chocolate.

Problems with direct and indirect objects

English and Spanish verbs with the same meaning usually take the same kind of object, but not always. The exceptions must be learned as vocabulary items. See the chart below for examples.

Comparison of objects in English and Spanish

INDIRECT OBJECT IN SPANISH	DIRECT OBJECT IN ENGLISH
Les duele.	It hurts **them**.
*José le enseñó a nadar a **Carlitos**.*	Joe taught **Charlie** to swim.
*Le pedí un préstamo a **Juan**.*	I asked **John** for a loan.
Le tiene miedo.	He fears **you**.

DIRECT OBJECT IN SPANISH	OBJECT OF A PREPOSITION IN ENGLISH
*Miran **la televisión**.*	They are looking at **the television**.
*Elena busca **el libro**.*	Helen is looking for **the book**.
*Miguel espera **el tren**.*	Michael is waiting for **the train**.
*Ana escucha **la radio**.*	Anne listens to **the radio**.

Definition   Determiners are words that introduce nouns and their adjectives. They usually come first in a noun phrase.

> ***the*** *red book*
> ***a*** *tall boy*
> ***each*** *window*
> ***several*** *students*

Types   Many kinds of words can serve as determiners: definite articles, indefinite articles, partitives, numbers, and general words like *each, either,* and *several.* Some types of adjectives (possessives, demonstratives, and interrogatives) can also be determiners; these are discussed in Chapter 5.

Forms   The **definite article** is always written *the,* but it is pronounced like *thee* before words beginning with a vowel or silent *h* (*the book* vs. *the apple, the hour*). The **indefinite article** is *a* or *an* in the singular, *some* in the plural. *An* is used before words beginning with a vowel or silent *h.* Other forms of determiners do not change their spelling or pronunciation.

Uses   DEFINITE ARTICLES   *The* indicates a specific noun.

> ***The*** *book* (the one you wanted) *is on the table.*

INDEFINITE ARTICLES   *A/an* refers to any individual in a class.

> *I see **a** boy* (not a specific one).

OTHER DETERMINERS   The use of other determiners is governed by the meaning.

> ***some*** *boys*
> ***few*** *boys*
> ***several*** *boys*
> ***eight*** *boys*

Spanish Introducing determiners

Forms

DEFINITE ARTICLES The form of the Spanish definite article depends on the gender and number of its noun and, in the feminine singular, whether the noun begins with a stressed *a*.

	DEFINITE ARTICLE	BEFORE STRESSED *a*
MASCULINE SINGULAR	*el*	
FEMININE SINGULAR	*la*	*el*
MASCULINE PLURAL	*los*	
FEMININE PLURAL	*las*	

These forms can also be combined with the prepositions *a* and *de* (see page 75).

INDEFINITE ARTICLES The indefinite article agrees with its noun in gender and number, just as the definite article does. "Some" expresses the plural of "a/an" in English; in Spanish, *unos/unas* express the plural of the singular indefinite articles *un/una*. Compare the forms below.

	INDEFINITE ARTICLE
MASCULINE SINGULAR	*un*
FEMININE SINGULAR	*una*
MASCULINE PLURAL	*unos*
FEMININE PLURAL	*unas*

OTHERS See also numbers, demonstrative and possessive adjectives, and indefinite words, all of which are used as determiners. Each indefinite word must be learned as a separate vocabulary item. Some determiners change spelling for gender or number; be sure to check as you learn new words.

siete	*mis*
este	*cada*
esas	*ninguno*
su	

Uses

Definite articles are used

1. before a specific noun, as in English.

2. before a noun used in a general sense.

*No me gusta **la** televisión.*	I hate television (generally speaking).
***La** guerra es mala.*	War (in general) is bad.

3. before many kinds of nouns that take no article in English.

LANGUAGES*	*el inglés*
QUALITIES	*la belleza*
SOME COUNTRIES†	*el Perú*
TITLES	*el general*
MODIFIED PROPER NAMES	*el viejo México*

---

* After certain verbs, such as *hablar* and *estudiar,* the article *el* is omitted.

† The countries whose names are most often preceded by a definite article are *el Canadá, los Estados Unidos, el Perú, el Paraguay, el Uruguay, el Ecuador, los Países Bajos, el Brasil,* and *el Japón.* Even these do not always require the article in spoken Spanish.

CONTINUED ON PAGE 18 ▶

Indefinite articles are used

1. for the number "one."

   un estudiante, **una** estudiante

2. for any member of a group or category.

   un grupo de estudiantes
   una buena profesora

3. for "some" members of a group or category.

   unos carros rojos
   unas ventanas

In Spanish, the indefinite article is sometimes omitted when used with the verb *ser* ("to be") to indicate a person's profession, nationality, occupation, or religion. If the noun is modified, however, an indefinite article is generally used.

Es profesor.	He is a teacher.
BUT	
*Es **un buen** profesor.*	He is a good teacher.
Es española.	She is a Spanish woman.
BUT	
*Es **una** española **muy guapa**.*	She is a very beautiful Spanish woman.
¿Es usted estudiante?	Are you a student?
BUT	
*¿Es usted **un buen** estudiante?*	Are you a good student?

OTHER DETERMINERS Most other Spanish determiners are used as they are in English. Exceptions are those that change to agree with the noun in gender and number. Differences are noted in dictionary entries.

4

Pronouns

Definition See page 6.

Forms Like nouns, English pronouns have gender, number, and case, but further distinctions can be made. They also show person.

PERSON English distinguishes three persons. **First person** is the one who is speaking (*I, me, we, us*). **Second person** is the one being spoken to (*you*). **Third person** is the one being spoken about (*he, him, she, her, it, they, them*). Both pronouns and verbs are listed according to person.

GENDER Some, but not all, pronouns can be distinguished by gender. *I* can refer to either a man or a woman. *She,* however, is always feminine, *he* always masculine, and *it,* even if it refers to an animal, is always neuter.

NUMBER Each of the three persons may be either singular or plural.

CASE Pronouns show more cases than nouns: the subjective (for example, *I* and *she*), the possessive (for example, *my/mine* and *her/hers*), and the objective (*me* and *her*). These are discussed below, under Uses.

Uses Personal pronouns have the same functions as nouns.

1. Subject

    ***She** is here.*

2. Direct object

    *I like **them**.*

3. Indirect object

    *I am giving **him** the book.*

4. Object of a preposition

    *The question is hard for **me**.*

5. Complement

    *It is **she** who is speaking.*

Types There are several types of pronouns.

1. Personal (page 22)

2. Possessive (page 28)

3. Reflexive/reciprocal (page 30)

4. Disjunctive (page 32)

5. Relative (page 34)

6. Demonstrative (page 38)

7. Interrogative (page 40)

Definitions, forms, and uses are the same for Spanish and English pronouns. However, there are a few important differences to be aware of.

In Spanish, the personal pronoun for "you" has two forms in the singular—the familiar *tú* and the formal *usted*. There are three forms in the plural—the familiar *vosotros* and *vosotras,* and the formal *ustedes.*

1. *Tú* is used to address the following.

   A family member of your generation
   Yourself
   A close friend
   A fellow student or colleague
   A child (under age 13)
   An inferior (sometimes as an insult)
   An animal
   God

   Usage varies in the different Spanish-speaking countries and cultures, however. In some places, *tú* can be used when you first meet someone, and in others it isn't appropriate to use *tú* until after you've gotten to know the person better. There are some regions where *tú* is hardly used at all.*

2. *Usted* is universally recognized in the Spanish-speaking world as the polite, or formal, way to say "you." *Usted* is often abbreviated as *Ud.* or *Vd.* Even though *usted* is used to address a second person, it uses third-person verb forms and pronouns. *Usted* is used for anyone not included in one of the categories listed for *tú,* especially those who are older than you are. Be careful: Unless the case is clear, use *usted* and allow the Spanish speaker to suggest using *tú.*

3. *Vosotros* and *vosotras* are plural forms corresponding to *tú* that can be used to address a group of people with whom you have a friendly relationship. These forms are used almost exclusively in Spain. You may come across these subject pronouns (or their object form, *os*) in your readings, but you are not expected to use them actively at this stage.

4. *Ustedes* is the plural form of *usted* and is often abbreviated as *Uds.* or *Vds.* It is the polite, or formal, way of addressing a group of people. It is also often used for plural "you" in less formal situations: *Ustedes* is used rather than *vosotros/vosotras* in most Spanish-speaking countries other than Spain; it is also used in some parts of Spain itself, especially in the south. Like *usted,* *ustedes* requires its verb and corresponding pronouns to be in the third person.

---

* A second-person singular pronoun used in place of *tú* in some regions of Latin America, especially Argentina, is *vos.* It is also widely used in many other countries, such as Uruguay, Paraguay, Colombia, and Guatemala. *Vos* is a familiar way of addressing an individual, like *tú,* but it uses different verb forms. In modern Spain, Mexico, the Caribbean, and other parts of Latin America, *vos* is no longer a part of everyday speech.

English Personal pronouns

Subject pronouns (see page 14)

	SINGULAR	PLURAL
FIRST PERSON	*I*	*we*
SECOND PERSON	*you*	*you*
THIRD PERSON	*he, she, it, one* (indefinite)	*they*

John gives a book. → ***He** gives it.* (third-person singular)
Mary and I arrive. → ***We** arrive.* (first-person plural)

Direct object pronouns (see page 14)

	SINGULAR	PLURAL
FIRST PERSON	*me*	*us*
SECOND PERSON	*you*	*you*
THIRD PERSON	*him, her, it, one*	*them*

*He sees **me**, and I see **you**.*
*You found **them**.*

CONTINUED ON PAGE 24 ▶

spanish Personal pronouns

Subject pronouns (see page 14)

In Spanish, a subject pronoun must always be of the same gender and number as the noun that it replaces.

	SINGULAR	PLURAL
FIRST PERSON	*yo*	*nosotros, nosotras*
SECOND PERSON	*tú*	*vosotros, vosotras*
THIRD PERSON	*él, ella, usted*	*ellos, ellas, ustedes*

The pronouns *él* and *ellos* refer only to males or, in the case of the plural form, possibly to a mixed group. The pronouns *ella* and *ellas* refer only to females.

> *Juan regala un libro.* → ***Él** lo regala.* (third-person singular)
> *María y yo llegamos.* → ***Nosotros** llegamos.* (first-person plural)

Direct object pronouns (see page 14)

	SINGULAR	PLURAL
FIRST PERSON	*me*	*nos*
SECOND PERSON	*te*	*os*
THIRD PERSON	*lo,* la*	*los, las*

*Él **me** ve, y yo **te** veo.*
*Usted **las** halló.*

For the third person, choosing the correct pronoun is easy if you remember that three of the pronouns (*la, los,* and *las*) are the same as the definite article. In the following example, the definite article and pronoun are *los*.

> *Busco **los** libros.* → ***Los** busco.*

POSITION Except in affirmative commands, an object pronoun in Spanish is placed directly before the conjugated verb of which it is the object.

*Él **me** ve. **Te** veo.*	He sees me. I see you.
*Busco el libro. **Lo** busco.*	I'm looking for the book. I'm looking for it.
*Juana compra los libros. Ella **los** compra.*	Juana buys the books. She buys them.
*No **lo** he visto.*	I have not seen it.

The object pronoun is also placed directly before the verb in a question or a negative sentence.

*¿Tienes los billetes? ¿**Los** tienes?*	Do you have the tickets? Do you have them?
*No tengo los billetes. No **los** tengo.*	I don't have the tickets. I don't have them.

O boletas
las

---

* In Spain and parts of Latin America, *le* is sometimes used instead of *lo* for the direct object pronoun "him."

CONTINUED ON PAGE 25 ▶

Indirect object pronouns (see page 14)

	SINGULAR	PLURAL
FIRST PERSON	*(to/for) me*	*(to/for) us*
SECOND PERSON	*(to/for) you*	*(to/for) you*
THIRD PERSON	*(to/for) him, her, it, one*	*(to/for) them*

*They send the letter **to us**.*
*He writes **her** a letter.*
*I bought a dress **for her**.*
*I got **them** a ticket.*

Objects of prepositions (see page 15)

After a preposition, English uses the same form of the pronoun as for direct objects.

Be careful with compound pronoun subjects or objects. These remain in the same case as that for a single subject or object.

*I am Spanish. **She** and **I** are Spanish.*
*This is between **us**. This is between **you** and **me**.*
*Give it to **them**. Give it to **him** and **her**.*

CONTINUED ON PAGE 26 ▶

The pronoun often follows infinitives and present participles and is attached to them.

Pedro quiere leer las cartas.	Peter wants to read the letters.
*Pedro **las** quiere leer.* OR *Pedro quiere leer**las**.*	Peter wants to read them.
*Están preparándo**los**.* OR ***Los** están preparando.*	They are preparing them.

The pronoun also follows and is attached to affirmative commands.

Dé el libro a María.	Give the book to Mary.
*Dé**lo** a María.*	Give it to Mary.

In negative commands, the pronoun is placed before the verb.

No dé el libro a María.	Don't give the book to Mary.
*No **lo** dé a María.*	Don't give it to Mary.

For more information about pronouns with commands, see page 115.

Indirect object pronouns (see page 14)

In Spanish, the indirect object is often used where English would use a preposition plus object.

	SINGULAR	PLURAL
FIRST PERSON	*me*	*nos*
SECOND PERSON	*te*	*os*
THIRD PERSON	*le*	*les*

The placement of indirect object pronouns is the same as for direct object pronouns.

*Él **le** escribe una carta.*	He is writing her a letter.
*No **me** envían una carta.*	They aren't sending me a letter.
*Mi mamá está preparándo**me** la cena.*	My mother is preparing dinner for me.
*Ellos quieren decir**te** un secreto.*	They want to tell you a secret.
*Di**me** la verdad.*	Tell me the truth.
*¡No **me** digas!*	Don't tell me! (You don't say!)

Objects of prepositions (see page 15)

Most prepositions require the disjunctive pronouns in Spanish (see page 33).

	SINGULAR	PLURAL
FIRST PERSON	*mí*	*nosotros, nosotras*
SECOND PERSON	*ti*	*vosotros, vosotras*
THIRD PERSON	*él, ella, usted*	*ellos, ellas, ustedes*

*Pienso **en ella**.*	I am thinking of her.
*Pensamos a menudo **en ti**.*	We often think of you.

There are special forms that combine object pronouns with the preposition *con*.

	SINGULAR	PLURAL
FIRST PERSON	*conmigo*	
SECOND PERSON	*contigo*	
THIRD PERSON	*consigo*	*consigo*

CONTINUED ON PAGE 27 ▶

WORD ORDER When there are two pronoun objects in English, the direct object comes before the indirect object.

*He shows **it to them**.*

When a noun and a pronoun are used together, word order can vary.

He shows	***the book***	***to them***.
	DIRECT OBJECT	INDIRECT OBJECT

He shows	***them***	***the book***.
	INDIRECT OBJECT	DIRECT OBJECT

WORD ORDER Spanish verbs may have more than one pronoun object.

> *Nos lo da.*   He gives **it to us**.

The order of pronouns before a verb is as follows.

> reflexive   indirect   direct

The indirect objects *le* and *les* become *se* when used before *lo, la, los,* and *las* (that is, when both the direct and the indirect objects are in the third person).

> *Pedro **le compra** los libros.*
> BUT
> ***Se los compra.***

Se has two uses. In addition to the use discussed above, *se* is also the reflexive pronoun "oneself." *Se* is always placed first, whether it is a reflexive, indirect, or direct object.

> ***Se lo** pone.*   He puts it on himself.
> ***Se lo** dan.*   They give it to her.

✓ QUICK CHECK

NORMAL SPANISH WORD ORDER

SUBJECT + PRONOUNS + VERB

me +	*lo*
nos	*la*
te	*los*
os	*las*
se	
le*	
les*	

In affirmative commands, the objects follow the verb. The indirect object comes before the direct object, regardless of person.

> *¡Démelo!*   Give it to me!
> *¡Muéstreselos!*   Show them to her!

For more information, see page 115.

---

* *Le* and *les* are used with the verb alone. They are replaced by *se* before *lo, la, los,* and *las.*

English Possessive pronouns

Definition A possessive pronoun replaces a possessive adjective (or a noun in the possessive) plus a noun.

> It's **my book**. → It's **mine**.
> It's **Anne's car**. → It's **hers**.

Forms Possessive pronouns have person and number; in the third-person singular, they also have gender. They do not have case, that is, they have the same form no matter what function they perform in a sentence.

	SINGULAR	PLURAL
FIRST PERSON	*mine*	*ours*
SECOND PERSON	*yours*	*yours*
THIRD PERSON	*his, hers, its, one's*	*theirs*

If you know the person, gender, and number of the possessor (*Mary* in the example below), there is only one choice for the pronoun (in this example, *hers*).

> *You have your book; where is **Mary's** book (**her** book)?*

To avoid repeating *book,* it is replaced along with the possessive noun or adjective in front of it. Since *Mary's* (or *her*) is third-person singular feminine, *hers* is the correct pronoun.

> *You have your book; where is **hers**?*

Spanish Possessive pronouns

Forms   In Spanish, possessive pronouns have person and number as in English, but they also have gender changes. Person indicates the possessor, while gender and number are determined by what is owned.

el libro de María	Mary's book	*las* camisas de Juan	John's shirts
su libro	her book	*sus* camisas	his shirts
el suyo	hers	*las suyas*	his

Even though *María* is female, the possessive pronoun is masculine singular (*el suyo*) because *libro* is masculine. Likewise, although *Juan* is male, *camisas* is feminine plural and therefore requires a feminine plural pronoun (*las suyas*).

*Es **el suyo**.*	It's hers.
*Son **las suyas**.*	They are his.

	SINGULAR	PLURAL
FIRST PERSON	*el mío, la mía, los míos, las mías*	*el nuestro, la nuestra, los nuestros, las nuestras*
SECOND PERSON	*el tuyo, la tuya, los tuyos, las tuyas*	*el vuestro, la vuestra, los vuestros, las vuestras*
THIRD PERSON	*el suyo, la suya, los suyos, las suyas*	*el suyo, la suya, los suyos, las suyas*

In Spanish, the possessive pronouns have the same forms, minus the definite article, as do the long forms of the possessive adjectives (see page 53).

Possessives may also be expressed in Spanish by using the definite article + *de* + the object pronoun in order to clarify the referent of *el suyo* or *la suya*.

Es su libro.	*Es el libro de usted.*	It is your book.
Es el suyo.	*Es el de usted.*	It is yours.
Es su libro.	*Es el libro de ella.*	It is her book.
Es el suyo.	*Es el de ella.*	It is hers.

Definition Reflexive pronouns are pronoun objects or complements that refer to the same person(s) or thing(s) as another element in the sentence, usually the subject.

Forms

	SINGULAR	PLURAL	RECIPROCAL
FIRST PERSON	*myself*	*ourselves*	*each other/one another*
SECOND PERSON	*yourself*	*yourselves*	*each other/one another*
THIRD PERSON	*himself, herself, itself, oneself*	*themselves*	*each other/one another*

Uses Reflexive pronouns are used as objects of verbs and prepositions.

Types A reflexive pronoun is normally used only when the subject acts directly on himself/herself or does something for himself/herself directly.

> *Paul cut **himself**.*
> *I told **myself** it didn't matter.*

Occasionally, reflexive pronouns are used idiomatically.

> *They always enjoy **themselves**.*

For mutual or reciprocal action, *each other* or *one another* is used. This expression does not change form.

> *They congratulated **each other**.*
> *You two saw **each other** last night.*

Reflexive pronouns can function as direct or indirect object pronouns.

> *They saw **each other**.*
> *We talked to **each other** yesterday.*

In English, reflexive and reciprocal objects are often omitted.

> *We **talked** yesterday. (To each other is understood.)*

Sometimes, a construction is used that requires no object.

> *Paul **got hurt**. (Hurt himself is understood.)*

However, consider the following sentence.

> *We washed this morning.*

If you have not heard the rest of the conversation, the meaning is ambiguous. The sentence may have either of the following meanings.

> *We washed ourselves (got washed).*
> *We washed our clothes (did the laundry).*

spanish Reflexive/reciprocal pronouns

Forms The forms of Spanish reflexive/reciprocal pronouns are the same as the forms of the direct and indirect object pronouns, except for the third person.

	SINGULAR	PLURAL
FIRST PERSON	*me*	*nos*
SECOND PERSON	*te*	*os*
THIRD PERSON	*se*	*se*

Reflexive/reciprocal pronouns are placed in the same position in a sentence as object pronouns.

Uses These pronouns are used as objects (either direct or indirect) of the verb (see pages 23, 25, and 27). They can be either reflexive, meaning "self," or reciprocal, meaning "each other."

Se hablan.	They are talking to themselves.
	OR They are talking to each other.

If the meaning is not clear, words can be added for clarification: A prepositional phrase that includes *mismo* or *propio* indicates the reflexive; *el uno al otro* indicates the reciprocal. Note that reflexive and reciprocal pronouns can function as direct and indirect object pronouns.

*Él **se** mira a sí mismo.* He is looking at himself.
    DIRECT OBJECT

*Se hablan **el uno al otro**.* They are talking to each other.
    INDIRECT OBJECT

Spanish uses many more reflexives than English, because transitive verbs must have objects in Spanish. Contrast the following sentences.

Lavamos el auto.	We wash the car.
Nos lavamos.	We wash ourselves.

Some Spanish verbs are reflexive in form only. With these verbs, use the reflexive pronoun in Spanish, but do not translate it.

Me acuesto.	I'm going to bed.
La mujer se acerca.	The woman is approaching.

Many Spanish verbs can be used either reflexively or nonreflexively. The meaning varies depending on the form, for example, *dormir* ("to sleep") and *dormirse* ("to fall asleep").

***Duermo** en la cama.*	I am sleeping in the bed.
***Me duermo** en la clase.*	I fall asleep in class.

Following is the present tense of the reflexive verb *dormirse*.

	SINGULAR	PLURAL
FIRST PERSON	*me duermo*	*nos dormimos*
SECOND PERSON	*te duermes*	*os dormís*
THIRD PERSON	*se duerme*	*se duermen*

English Disjunctive pronouns

Definition   A disjunctive pronoun is not attached to a verb. (*Disjunctive* means "not joined.") It is used alone or as an extra word to give special emphasis or to intensify an impression.

Forms and uses   The form of a disjunctive pronoun depends on its use.

1. Used alone, the disjunctive pronoun is in the subjective case (if required) in formal English, and in the objective case for informal use.

    Who's there? **I**. (formal; *I am* is understood)
    　　　　　　　Me. (informal)

2. As an intensifier, the reflexive pronoun is normally used.

    I'll do it **myself**!
    He told me so **himself**.

3. Sometimes, we merely raise our voices for emphasis.

    You *do it!*

Spanish Disjunctive pronouns

Forms Spanish disjunctive pronouns have the following forms.

	SINGULAR	PLURAL
FIRST PERSON	*mí**	*nosotros, nosotras*
SECOND PERSON	*ti*	*vosotros, vosotras*
THIRD PERSON	*él, ella, usted*	*ellos, ellas, ustedes*
	sí (reflexive)	*sí* (reflexive)

Uses Disjunctive pronouns may be used

1. alone.

   *¿Quién es? ¡**Yo**!* Who is it? **Me**!

2. with *mismo* for emphasis.

   *Yo **mismo** voy a hacerlo.* I'm going to do it **myself**.

3. after prepositions.

   *Eso es **para mí**.* That is **for me**.

When used with the preposition *con* ("with"), *mí, ti,* and *sí* are replaced by *-migo, -tigo,* and *-sigo* to create special forms: *conmigo, contigo, consigo.*

   *Hable **conmigo**.* Talk with me.

---

*The disjunctive pronoun *mí* has an accent to distinguish it from the possessive adjective *mi* (see page 53).

English Relative pronouns

Definition Relative pronouns begin a relative clause. They refer to a noun, called the antecedent, and usually come directly after that noun.

Forms Relative pronouns have the following forms in English.

	SUBJECT	OBJECT	POSSESSIVE	INDIRECT OBJECT/PREPOSITIONAL OBJECT
PERSON	*who/that*	*whom/that*	*whose*	*to/by whom*
THING	*which/that*	*which/that*	*whose/*	*to/by which*
			of which	*where* (for place prepositions)
				when (for time prepositions)

The correct pronoun is determined by the following factors.

1. Whether the antecedent is a person or a thing

2. The function of the pronoun in the clause

3. For subjects and objects, whether the clause is restrictive or nonrestrictive

   A **restrictive clause** defines the noun. *That* is used, and the clause is not set off by commas.

   > The book **that** *you just read is world-renowned.*

   Without the clause, you would not know which book is meant. It is an essential definition.

   A **nonrestrictive clause** describes the noun, rather than defines it. It is not necessary to form a complete sentence. *Who, whom,* or *which* is used, and the clause is set off by commas.

   > Don Quijote, **which** *the class is going to read, is very famous.*

   The relative clause could be eliminated, and the sentence would still make sense. It is a nonessential description.

Uses Relative pronouns have several uses.

1. They introduce clauses that give additional information about the antecedent.

2. They allow you to join two short sentences to make your writing smoother and to avoid repetition.

   > *Enrique González came yesterday. Enrique González is an expert pianist.*
   > → *Enrique González,* **who** *is an expert pianist, came yesterday.*

3. They can be subjects, direct objects, indirect objects, possessives, or objects of a preposition in the relative clause.

4. They are inflected only for case, not for person or number. Their form depends on their function in the clause.

   The function of the antecedent in the main clause has no effect on the form of the relative pronoun.

Spanish Relative pronouns

Forms   Relative pronouns have the following forms in Spanish.

	SUBJECT	OBJECT	PREPOSITIONAL OBJECT	OTHER
PERSON	que	que el cual*	quien, quienes	cuyo, cuya
THING	que	que	que	

Unlike English, Spanish does not use different pronouns to distinguish between restrictive and nonrestrictive clauses.

*El libro **que usted acaba de leer** es famoso.*	The book **that you have just read** is famous.
*Don Quijote, **que la clase va a leer**, es una novela famosa.*	*Don Quijote*, **which the class is going to read**, is a famous novel.

Relative pronouns are often omitted in English, but Spanish does not allow this.

*Es el hombre **que** vi ayer.*	That's the man I saw yesterday. ("whom" is omitted)

All relative pronouns must have antecedents. If there isn't one, *lo* is supplied. In the following example, "which" does not refer to any specific noun, but to the idea (or fact) that he did not come.

*No llegó, **lo cual** me sorprendió.*	He didn't come, which surprised me.

A relative pronoun can take any form of the verb in its clause. This is also true of English, but many people do not follow this practice.

*Soy yo **que soy** ansioso.*	It is I **who am** worried.
*Somos nosotros **que venimos**.*	We are the ones **who are coming**.

---

*These forms must agree in gender and number with their antecedent, although only the masculine singular is given here. These forms are generally used if you need to distinguish gender or number, for example, if there are two nouns to which the relative pronoun could refer. Remember to use contractions with *a* and *de,* such as *al cual* and *del cual* (see page 75).

How to analyze relative pronouns

Mr. Smith *is **an excellent cook***.		***Mr. Smith*** *made **these pies***.	
SUBJECT	COMPLEMENT	SUBJECT	DIRECT OBJECT

1. Find the repeated element. → *Mr. Smith*
2. Find the function of the repeated element in the second sentence, which will become the relative clause. → the subject
3. Choose the relative pronoun. → *who* (person, subject)
4. Copy the first sentence through the antecedent. → *Mr. Smith* . . .
5. Put in the correct relative pronoun, in this case, *who.* → *Mr. Smith, who* . . .
6. Copy the relative clause. → *Mr. Smith, who made these pies* . . .
7. Copy the rest of the first sentence. Leave out any parts represented by the relative pronoun. → *Mr. Smith, who made these pies, is an excellent cook.*

Other examples follow.

The ten books are on the table. I am reading them.
*The ten books **that** I am reading are on the table.*

> *That* is used because it
>
> 1. is the object of *am reading* in the clause (no commas).
> 2. refers to a thing.
> 3. is restrictive (defines which ten books).

Mr. Jones died today. I saw him yesterday.
*Mr. Jones, **whom** I saw yesterday, died today.*

> *Whom* is used because it
>
> 1. is the object of *I saw* (with commas).
> 2. refers to a person.
> 3. is nonrestrictive. (You already know who Mr. Jones is. This merely gives an extra fact about him.)

The student is asleep. I am speaking to that student.
*The student **to whom** I am speaking is asleep.*

> *To whom* is used because it
>
> 1. is the indirect object (no commas).
> 2. refers to a person.
> 3. is restrictive (defines which student).

The old house is falling down. I lived in that house as a child.
*The old house **where** (in which) I lived as a child is falling down.*

> *Where* is used because it
>
> 1. replaces a place preposition plus noun object (no commas).
> 2. refers to a thing. (*In which* is also correct.)

The woman lives in New York. I took her coat.
*The woman **whose** coat I took lives in New York.*

> *Whose* is used because it
>
> 1. is possessive (no commas).
> 2. refers to a person.
> 3. is restrictive (defines which woman).

Spanish How to analyze relative pronouns

The important considerations are function in the clause and word order.

> **La señora Sánchez** *es* **una periodista excelente**.
> SUBJECT   COMPLEMENT

> **La señora Sánchez** *escribió* **estos ensayos**.
> SUBJECT   DIRECT OBJECT

1. Find the repeated element. → *La señora Sánchez*

2. Identify the function of the repeated element in the second sentence, which will become the relative clause. → the subject

3. Choose the relative pronoun. → *que*

4. Copy the first sentence through the noun phrase to be described. → *La señora Sánchez…*

5. Put in the relative pronoun (with preposition, if any) to replace the second *La señora Sánchez*. → *La señora Sánchez, que…*

6. Copy the rest of the second sentence (now a relative clause). → *La señora Sánchez, que escribió estos ensayos,…*

7. Copy the rest of the first sentence. → *La señora Sánchez, que escribió estos ensayos, es una periodista excelente.*

Try this with other sentences. Follow the same steps until they feel natural.

> *Los diez libros están en la mesa. Los estoy leyendo.*
> *Los diez libros que estoy leyendo están en la mesa.*

> *El señor Pérez murió hoy. Lo vi ayer.*
> *El señor Pérez, al que vi ayer, murió hoy.*

> *El estudiante está durmiendo. Hablo con este estudiante.*
> *El estudiante a quien hablo está durmiendo.*

> *La vieja casa se derrumbó. Vivía yo en esta casa durante mi juventud.*
> *La vieja casa en la cual vivía durante mi juventud se derrumbó.*

> *La mujer vive en Nueva York. Llevé la chaqueta de esa mujer.*
> *La mujer de quien llevé la chaqueta vive en Nueva York.*

This may seem complicated, requiring a lot of thought. That is because people usually use many short sentences when speaking. Relative clauses are used mainly to vary written style—when you have time to think, cross something out, and write it in a different way.

English Demonstrative pronouns

Definition   Demonstrative pronouns point out someone or something.

Forms   There are four forms of the demonstrative pronoun in English.

SINGULAR	PLURAL
this (one)	*these*
that (one)	*those*

Uses   These pronouns distinguish only between what is near (*this, these*) and far (*that, those*) and between singular and plural. No changes are made for gender or case.

> *I can't decide which of the chairs to buy.*
> ***This one*** *is lovely, but* ***that one*** *is comfortable.*
> ***This*** *is lovely, but* ***that*** *is comfortable.*

Spanish Demonstrative pronouns

Forms   The forms of the demonstrative pronouns in Spanish follow.

		SINGULAR	PLURAL
GROUP I	MASCULINE	*éste, ése*	*éstos, ésos*
	FEMININE	*ésta, ésa*	*éstas, ésas*
	NEUTER	*esto, eso*	
GROUP II	MASCULINE	*aquél*	*aquéllos*
	FEMININE	*aquélla*	*aquéllas*
	NEUTER	*aquello*	

With the exception of the neuter forms *esto, eso,* and *aquello,* all of the demonstrative pronouns carry a written accent on the stressed vowel to distinguish them from the demonstrative adjectives (*este, aquel,* etc.).

Uses   A demonstrative pronoun replaces a demonstrative adjective plus its noun.

este hombre → éste   *aquel hombre → aquél*
esa mujer → ésa   *aquella mujer → aquélla*
estos niños → éstos   *aquellos niños → aquéllos*
estas niñas → éstas   *aquellas niñas → aquéllas*

The forms *éste* and *ésta* usually translate as English "this one," and *éstos* and *éstas* usually translate as "these."

Forms of both *ése* and *aquél* translate as "that," but *aquél* implies greater distance ("that one over there"). *Ésos* and *aquéllos* translate respectively as "those" and "those over there."

Esto and *eso* are used to translate the English indefinite pronouns "this" and "that." *Aquello* translates as the indefinite "that over there."

Demonstrative pronouns are also used to indicate "the former" (forms of *aquél*) and "the latter" (forms of *éste*).

Remember that the masculine and feminine forms of the demonstrative pronoun (used without the noun) are distinguished from the equivalent demonstrative adjective (used with a noun) by a written accent placed on the stressed vowel.

☑ QUICK CHECK

	DEMONSTRATIVE ADJECTIVE + NOUN	DEMONSTRATIVE PRONOUN
SINGULAR	*este libro, aquel libro*	*éste, aquél*
	esta casa, aquella casa	*ésta, aquélla*
PLURAL	*estos papeles, aquellos papeles*	*éstos, aquéllos*
	estas cartas, aquellas cartas	*éstas, aquéllas*
NEUTER		*esto, eso, aquello*

English Interrogative pronouns

Definition   Interrogative pronouns ask a question.

Forms   Interrogative pronouns have different forms for people and things. The pronoun referring to people, *who*, is also inflected for case.

	PEOPLE	THINGS
SUBJECT	*who?*	*which?* *what?*
OBJECT	*whom?*	*which?* *what?*

No change is made for number. *Who?/whom?* and *what?* can refer to one or more than one.

Uses   The interrogative pronouns in English are used in the following ways.

1. Person as subject

   Who *is coming? John.* OR *The Smiths.*

2. Thing as subject

   What *is going on? A riot.*

3. Person as direct object

   Whom *did you see? John.*

4. Thing as direct object

   What *are you doing? My homework.*

5. Person as indirect object*

   To whom *are you speaking? To Mary.*

6. Person as object of a preposition

   With whom *are you going? With Felipe.*

7. Thing as object of a preposition

   What *are you thinking* **about**? *About the music.*

As an interrogative pronoun, *which?* relates to choice. It can simply be *which?*, used in the singular or plural, or *which one(s)?*

   Here are two books. **Which (one)** *do you want?*
   There are many good shops in town. **Which (ones)** *do you like best?*

---

* To or *for* signals the indirect object. (To review the indirect object, see page 14.)

spanish Interrogative pronouns

Forms Interrogative pronouns are confusing in both English and Spanish, because the forms are used for other purposes. They are more complex in Spanish, however, because in most cases you have a choice of forms.

	SINGULAR	PLURAL	ENGLISH EQUIVALENT
PERSON	*¿quién?*	*¿quiénes?*	who? whom?
THING	*¿qué?*	*¿qué?*	what?

For the differences in usage between *¿qué?* and *¿cuál?*, see Appendix A.

Uses In formal English, many speakers make a distinction between "who?" (subject of a verb) and "whom?" (object of a verb). Spanish does not do this. *¿Quién?* and *¿quiénes?* can function as either the subject or object of a verb.

The English interrogative pronoun "what?" can function as either subject of a verb or object of a verb or preposition. It does not have different forms for gender or number.

The Spanish interrogative pronoun *¿qué?* can function as either subject of a verb or object of a verb or preposition. This is also the case for *¿cuál?*, whose forms also show gender and number.

The interrogative pronouns in Spanish are used in the following ways.

1. Person as subject

   *¿**Quién** llega? María.*
   *¿**Quiénes** llegan? Juan y María.*

2. Thing as subject

   *¿**Qué** pasa? Nada.*

3. Person as direct object

   *¿**A quiénes** vio usted? A Lola y a Tomás.*

4. Thing as direct object

   *¿**Qué** haces? Leo el periódico.*

5. Person as indirect object

   *¿**A quién** hablabas? A María.*

6. Person as object of a preposition

   *¿**Con quién** va usted al cine? Con Jesús.*

7. Thing as object of a preposition

   *¿**En qué** piensa usted? En la música.*

In Spanish, the direct object form of the interrogative pronoun is preceded by the preposition *a*, just as a direct object noun indicating a person is.

CONTINUED ON PAGE 42 ▶

Choice interrogatives

Another kind of interrogative pronoun relates to choice: "Which one(s)?" These forms agree in gender and number with the noun they replace.

	SINGULAR	ENGLISH EQUIVALENT	PLURAL	ENGLISH EQUIVALENT
PERSON	*¿cuál?*	which one?	*¿cuáles?*	which ones?
THING	*¿cuál?*	which one?	*¿cuáles?*	which ones?
MASCULINE	*¿cuánto?*	how much?	*¿cuántos?*	how many?
FEMININE	*¿cuánta?*	how much?	*¿cuántas?*	how many?

These interrogatives offer a choice between possibilities.

*Tengo tres **periódicos**. ¿**Cuál** prefieres?*

*Hay muchas **tiendas** cerca de la plaza. ¿**Cuáles** prefieren Uds.?*

5

Adjectives

English Introducing adjectives

Definition   See page 7.

Forms   Some English adjectives are invariable, while others change form. These changes depend on adjective type. The types are discussed separately below.

Uses   Adjectives are primarily used as

1. modifiers of nouns or pronouns.

2. complements of either the subject or an object.

An adjective's function determines its position in a sentence.

1. As a modifier, an adjective usually comes before the noun or pronoun that it modifies.

   *Buy **that small white house**.*
   ADJECTIVES   NOUN

   *Buy the **blue**   one.*
   ADJECTIVE PRONOUN

2. As a modifier of an indefinite pronoun, an adjective follows the pronoun.

   Something   ***terrible** is happening.*
   INDEFINITE PRONOUN ADJECTIVE

3. As a subject complement, an adjective follows the verb *to be* or the linking verb and describes the subject.

   *Mrs. López **is**   **happy**.*
   FORM OF *to be*   ADJECTIVE

   *They **seem**   **pleased**.*
   LINKING VERB   ADJECTIVE

4. As an object complement, an adjective follows the direct object noun or pronoun.

   *That made **the exam hard**.*
   NOUN   ADJECTIVE

   *We considered **him**   **crazy**.*
   PRONOUN   ADJECTIVE

Types   Each of the following adjective types is discussed separately below.

1. Descriptive (page 46)

2. Proper (a kind of descriptive adjective) (page 50)

3. Limiting (includes demonstratives, possessives, indefinites, interrogatives, numbers, and determiners) (page 50)

Spanish Introducing adjectives

Forms An adjective in Spanish agrees in gender and number with the noun it modifies. If an adjective describes a mixed group of nouns (masculine and feminine), the adjective is masculine plural.

Uses As in English, Spanish adjectives are used as modifiers and complements, but their position in a sentence is different (see page 47).

English Descriptive adjectives

Definition   Descriptive adjectives describe a noun or pronoun.

Forms   Many of these adjectives may be inflected to show comparison.

Spanish Descriptive adjectives

Forms   In Spanish, descriptive adjectives that are masculine singular typically end in -o, and feminine singular descriptive adjectives typically end in -a. Plurals are created by adding an -s. The masculine singular form is the one listed first in vocabularies and dictionaries.

	SINGULAR	PLURAL
MASCULINE	*bueno*	*buenos*
FEMININE	*buena*	*buenas*

1. Most descriptive adjectives whose singular forms do not end in -o or -a have a single form. The plural is formed by adding -es unless the descriptive adjective already ends in -e, in which case -s is added to form the plural.

SINGULAR	PLURAL	ENGLISH EQUIVALENT	ADJECTIVES FOLLOWING THIS PATTERN
fácil	*fáciles*	easy	*difícil, útil, real*
feroz	*feroces*	ferocious	*audaz, capaz, sagaz*
doble	*dobles*	double	*pobre, grande, verde*

Note that spelling changes are employed to maintain pronunciation.

2. Adjectives ending in -án, -ón, -ín, and -or add -a for the feminine. Masculine plurals add -es, and feminine plurals are formed by adding -s.

SINGULAR		PLURAL	
MASCULINE	FEMININE	MASCULINE	FEMININE
catalán	*catalana*	*catalanes*	*catalanas*
mandón	*mandona*	*mandones*	*mandonas*
saltarín	*saltarina*	*saltarines*	*saltarinas*
hablador	*habladora*	*habladores*	*habladoras*

3. Comparative forms of adjectives ending in -or (*superior, ulterior,* etc.) have the same form in the masculine and feminine.

SINGULAR		PLURAL	
MASCULINE	FEMININE	MASCULINE	FEMININE
superior	*superior*	*superiores*	*superiores*

4. Adjectives indicating nationality that end in a consonant form the feminine and feminine plural regularly; the masculine plural ends in -es.

SINGULAR		PLURAL	
MASCULINE	FEMININE	MASCULINE	FEMININE
andaluz	*andaluza*	*andaluces*	*andaluzas*
español	*española*	*españoles*	*españolas*
portugués	*portuguesa*	*portugueses*	*portuguesas*
inglés	*inglesa*	*ingleses*	*inglesas*

CONTINUED ON PAGE 47 ▶

5. A small group of adjectives (not just descriptive adjectives) have a shortened form that is used before masculine singular nouns.

alguno → *algún*	***algún*** *libro*
ninguno → *ningún*	***ningún*** *libro*
bueno → *buen*	***buen*** *tiempo*
malo → *mal*	***mal*** *tiempo*
primero → *primer*	*el **primer** mes*
tercero → *tercer*	*el **tercer** mes*
uno → *un*	***un*** *día*
Santo → *San*	***San*** *Juan*
BUT	

Santo *Domingo,* ***Santo*** *Tomás, and el **santo** padre*

6. The adjective *grande* becomes *gran* before most singular nouns of either gender; its meaning then becomes "great" rather than "big."

> *un **gran** amigo, una **gran** amiga*

7. If two adjectives that have a short form are used before a singular noun, they both use the short form unless they are connected by a conjunction, such as *y* ("and").

> *un **mal** tiempo, el **primer buen** día, el primero y **buen** disco*

WORD ORDER Normally, a descriptive adjective in Spanish follows the noun it modifies. First, you say what you're talking about (for example, *una casa*), then you describe it (for example, *una casa blanca*).

1. Some adjectives change meaning, depending on whether they appear before or after the noun.

ADJECTIVE	MEANING BEFORE	MEANING AFTER
antiguo, antigua	ancient	former
cierto, cierta	some	definite
diferente	unalike	various
nuevo, nueva	another	brand-new
pobre	pitiable	not rich
viejo, vieja	long-standing	aged

2. There are a number of Spanish adjectives whose English equivalent has the same meaning, but whose placement in Spanish offers a variation in connotation. In these cases the position before the noun suggests an inherent quality.

la blanca nieve	white snow (snow is naturally white)
la nieve gris	gray snow (the normally white snow has been made gray)

3. When two descriptive adjectives are used together to modify a noun, the one most closely associated with the noun comes first.

la pintura mexicana moderna	modern Mexican painting

4. It is important to place adjectives appropriately.

*el **famoso** presidente **norteamericano**, Abraham Lincoln*	the **great American** president, Abraham Lincoln
*la **gran** escritora **chilena contemporánea**, Isabel Allende*	the **great contemporary Chilean** writer, Isabel Allende
*el cuento **místico e interesante***	the **mystical and interesting** story
*la ciudad **grande y hermosa***	the **big and beautiful** city

English Comparison of adjectives

Definition The three degrees of comparison are positive, comparative, and superlative.

Forms English forms comparisons in the following ways.

1. Regular comparisons add -er and -est to short adjectives, sometimes with a minor change in spelling.

   *short ~ short**er** ~ short**est***
   *pretty ~ prett**ier** ~ prett**iest***

2. Longer adjectives are compared by using *more* and *most,* or the negatives *less* and *least.*

   *determined ~ **more** determined ~ **most** determined*
   *obvious ~ **less** obvious ~ **least** obvious*

3. Some adjectives have irregular comparisons.

   good ~ better ~ best
   bad ~ worse ~ worst

4. Adjectives that cannot be compared include absolutes, which are by definition superlative. Uniqueness and perfection cannot be brought to a higher degree.

   unique
   perfect

5. When a comparison is made, several words may introduce the second element: *than, in,* and *of all.*

   COMPARATIVE *He is taller **than** I (am).*
   SUPERLATIVE *He is the tallest **in** the class. He is the tallest **of all** my students.*

If an adjective is already in the comparative, *more* is not added. Greater contrast may be expressed by words like *much* or *more.*

   ***much** smaller*
   ***much** more difficult*

Spanish Comparison of adjectives

Forms Spanish forms comparisons in the following ways.

1. Most Spanish adjectives form the comparative with *más* ("more"), *tan* ("as," in the sense of equal), or *menos* ("less") plus the adjective.

   *grande ~ **más** grande ~ **tan** grande ~ **menos** grande*
   *importante ~ **más** importante ~ **tan** importante ~ **menos** importante*

2. Superlatives are formed with the definite article plus the comparative (for example, *la más grande* and *el menos importante*).

   *un auto **rápido** ~ un auto **más rápido** ~ el auto **más rápido** OR **el más rápido***
   *una camisa **bonita** ~ una camisa **menos bonita** ~ la camisa **menos bonita***
       OR ***la menos bonita***

CONTINUED ON PAGE 49 ▶

The adjective remains in the same position, whether it is positive, comparative, or superlative.

*Es una casa **grande**.* (positive)	It is a big house.
*Es una casa **más grande**.* (comparative)	It is a bigger house.
*Es **la** casa **más grande**.*	It is the biggest house.
OR *Es **la más grande**.* (superlative)	OR It is the biggest (house).

1. The most common irregular comparisons are the following.

bueno ~ mejor	better
malo ~ peor	worse
grande ~ mayor OR *más grande*	greater, bigger
pequeño ~ menor OR *más pequeño*	lesser, smaller

2. Adjectives that cannot be compared include absolutes, which are by definition superlative.

único, única	unique
perfecto, perfecta	perfect

Since uniqueness and perfection cannot be brought to a higher degree, *el/la/los/las más* cannot be used with them.

3. To link elements in a comparison, use *que* with *más* ("more") or *menos* ("less"), and use *como* with *tan* ("as," in the sense of equal).

Jimena es más grande que María.
Marco es menos grande que Felipe.
Juan es tan grande como yo.

For a superlative, use *de* to compare one to a group.

Jimena es la más grande de su familia.
Felipe es el más grande de su clase.

✓ QUICK CHECK

COMPARATIVE CONSTRUCTION WITH (1) *los hombres*, (2) *las mujeres*, AND (3) *ser inteligente*

NOUN 1	+ VERB	+ COMPARATIVE	+ ADJECTIVE	+ *que*	+ NOUN 2
Los hombres	*son*	*más*	*inteligentes*	*que*	*las mujeres.*
Los hombres	*son*	*tan*	*inteligentes*	*como*	*las mujeres.*
Los hombres	*son*	*menos*	*inteligentes*	*que*	*las mujeres.*

SUPERLATIVE CONSTRUCTION WITH (1) *Consuelo*, (2) *la clase*, AND (3) *ser lista*

NOUN 1	+ VERB	+ SUPERLATIVE	+ ADJECTIVE	+ *de*	+ NOUN 2
Consuelo	*es*	*la más*	*lista*	*de*	*la clase.*

Note that nouns may be replaced by noun phrases or pronouns.

Make sure that the word order is correct, that there is subject-verb agreement, and that the adjective agrees with the noun or pronoun it modifies.

Definition   A proper adjective is a descriptive adjective formed from a proper noun (see page 12).

NOUN	ADJECTIVE
Rome	*Roman*
Shakespeare	*Shakespearean*

Forms   In English, both proper nouns and their adjectives are capitalized. Sometimes, their forms are indistinguishable.

NOUN	ADJECTIVE
the Spanish	*the Spanish people*

English Limiting adjectives

Definition   A limiting adjective does not add to your knowledge of a noun; instead, it directs you toward the right one by limiting the choices. The following examples show the types of limiting adjectives.

DEMONSTRATIVE	***this*** *chapter* (not another one)
POSSESSIVE	***his*** *book* (not hers)
INTERROGATIVE	***whose*** *coat?* (its specific owner)
INDEFINITE	***some*** *people* (but not others)
ORDINAL NUMBER	*the* ***second*** *lesson* (not the first)

Each of these types of limiting adjectives are discussed separately.

English Demonstrative adjectives

Definition   Demonstrative adjectives point out which of a group is/are the one(s) that you are referring to.

Forms   These adjectives have the same forms as the demonstrative pronouns (see page 38) and distinguish in the same way between near and far and between singular and plural.

	SINGULAR	PLURAL
NEAR	*this*	*these*
FAR	*that*	*those*

There is no agreement in person, gender, or case. The demonstrative adjective precedes its noun.

*****This*** *woman is talking to* ***that*** *man.*
*****These*** *little boys hate* ***those*** *dogs.*

ꜱpᴀɴiꜱʜ Proper adjectives

Forms In Spanish, proper adjectives are formed from proper nouns, but they are not capitalized.

NOUN	ADJECTIVE	ENGLISH EQUIVALENT
un romano	*la gente romana*	**Roman**
un venezolano	*la gente venezolana*	**Venezuelan**

ꜱpᴀɴiꜱʜ Limiting adjectives

See the discussion on the opposite page.

ꜱpᴀɴiꜱʜ Demonstrative adjectives

Forms A demonstrative adjective agrees with the noun it modifies in gender and number.

SINGULAR		PLURAL	
MASCULINE	FEMININE	MASCULINE	FEMININE
este	*esta*	*estos*	*estas*
ese	*esa*	*esos*	*esas*
aquel	*aquella*	*aquellos*	*aquellas*

Uses In Spanish, the near/far distinction is expressed by the forms *este/ese/aquel. Este/esta* ("this") and *estos/estas* ("these") express what is nearest to the speaker; *ese/esa* ("that") and *esos/esas* ("those") express what is farther from the speaker; and *aquel/aquella* ("that over there") and *aquellos/aquellas* ("those over there") express what is farthest from the speaker. Use forms of *ese* for "that" unless it is necessary to make a point of the distinction.

aquella *mujer*	**that** woman (over there)
esa *mujer*	**that** woman (as opposed to **this** woman)

*Esta mujer hablaba con **ese** hombre.*	**This** woman was talking with **that** man.
*Este hombre ama a **aquella** mujer.*	**This** man loves **that** woman (over there).

English Possessive adjectives

Definition Possessive adjectives modify a noun by telling to whom or what it belongs.

Forms These adjectives indicate the person, number, and gender (in the third-person singular) of the *possessor*.

	SINGULAR	PLURAL
FIRST PERSON	*my*	*our*
SECOND PERSON	*your*	*your*
THIRD PERSON	*his, her, its, one's*	*their*

The adjectives do not tell anything about the person or thing that is possessed.

Mr. García's *son* → **his** *son* (third-person singular masculine)
Mrs. García's *son* → **her** *son* (third-person singular feminine)
the Garcías' *son* → **their** *son* (third-person plural)

Uses The possessive adjective is always used with the noun.

my *mother*
our *child*
your *turn*

If the noun is omitted, a pronoun must be used (for example, *mine, ours,* or *yours*) (see page 28).

spanish Possessive adjectives

Definition Spanish possessives are adjectives, so they agree in gender and number with the noun they modify, *not* with the possessor.

Forms Spanish possessive adjectives have the following forms.

		SINGULAR	PLURAL	ENGLISH EQUIVALENT
SINGULAR	FIRST PERSON	*mi*	*mis*	my
	SECOND PERSON	*tu*	*tus*	your
	THIRD PERSON	*su*	*sus*	his, her, its, your
PLURAL	FIRST PERSON	*nuestro, nuestra*	*nuestros, nuestras*	our
	SECOND PERSON	*vuestro, vuestra*	*vuestros, vuestras*	your
	THIRD PERSON	*su*	*sus*	their, your

The adjectives *mi/mis/tu/tus/su/sus* indicate singular and plural, but they do not indicate gender.

The adjectives *nuestro/nuestra/nuestros/nuestras/vuestro/vuestra/vuestros/vuestras* indicate both gender and number.

The adjectives *su/sus* have several English equivalents ("his," "her," "its," "your," "their"). Therefore context may clarify which English possessive adjective is indicated. If context is not clear, use *de* + a noun or pronoun for clarification.

> *su libro*   *el libro de María* OR *el libro de ella*

English "your" has several Spanish equivalents, depending on the subject of the Spanish sentence. It is expressed by *su/sus* if the subject of the Spanish verb is *usted* or *ustedes*; by *tu/tus* if the subject is *tú*; and by *vuestro/vuestra/vuestros/vuestras* if the subject of the verb is *vosotros* or *vosotras*.

In Spanish, to stress the possessive adjective, use the long form of the Spanish possessive adjective.

SINGULAR	PLURAL
mío, mía, míos, mías	*nuestro, nuestra, nuestros, nuestras*
tuyo, tuya, tuyos, tuyas	*vuestro, vuestra, vuestros, vuestras*
suyo, suya, suyos, suyas	*suyo, suya, suyos, suyas*

This form of the possessive adjective is placed after the noun.

> *mi amigo*   my friend   *el amigo mío*   **my** friend OR friend **of mine**

English Interrogative adjectives

Definition   Interrogative adjectives ask a question about limitation.

Forms   These adjectives have case in English.

1. Subject and object cases: *which? what?*

2. Possessive case: *whose?*

These forms are invariable.

Uses   Interrogative adjectives are used

1. to ask a question.

SUBJECT	***What** assignment is for today?*
OBJECT	***Which** class do you have at 10 o'clock?*
POSSESSIVE	***Whose** coat is this?*

2. in an exclamation.

***What** a pretty house!*
***What** a job!*

English Indefinite adjectives

Definition   Indefinite adjectives refer to nouns or pronouns that are not defined more specifically.

***Some** students learn fast.*
***Any** girl will tell you.*
***Both** lectures are at 10 o'clock.*
***Each/Every** class has its value.*
*I want **another** pen.*
***Such** behavior is terrible.*

Forms   These adjectives are invariable, that is, they do not change their form. Some, however, may be used only with singular nouns (for example, *each, every, another*), some only with plural nouns (for example, *both, other*), and some with either singular or plural nouns (for example, *some: some coffee, some people*).

spanish Interrogative adjectives

Forms In Spanish, the interrogative adjective is inflected for gender and number. It agrees with the noun it modifies.

| SINGULAR | | PLURAL | | |
MASCULINE	FEMININE	MASCULINE	FEMININE	ENGLISH EQUIVALENT
¿qué?	¿qué?	¿qué?	¿qué?	which? what?
¿cuál?	¿cuál?	¿cuáles?	¿cuáles?	which?
¿cuánto?	¿cuánta?	¿cuántos?	¿cuántas?	how much? how many?

The interrogative adjective *¿qué?* has only one form and therefore does not indicate gender or number.

The interrogative adjective *¿cuál?* indicates number but not gender.

¿Cuánto?/¿cuánta? ("how much?") and *¿cuántos?/¿cuántas?* ("how many?") indicate both gender and number.

Uses Interrogative adjectives are used

1. to ask a question.

   *¿**Cuántos** libros tienes?*
   *¿**Qué** hora es?*
   *¿**Qué** trabajo tenemos para mañana?*
   *¿**Cuál** es el trabajo para mañana?*

2. in an exclamation.

   *¡**Qué** casa más bonita!*
   *¡**Qué** lío!*

spanish Indefinite adjectives

Definition Spanish indefinite adjectives are similar to those in English.

***Algunos** estudiantes aprenden rápidamente.*
***Cualquier** mujer se lo dirá a usted.*
***Ambas** conferencias se reúnen a las diez.*
***Cada** clase tiene valor.*
*Quisiera **otro** bolígrafo.*
***Tal** comportamiento es reprensible.*

Forms An indefinite adjective agrees with its noun in gender and number, just as descriptive adjectives do.

English Other limiting adjectives

Ordinal numbers

These numbers indicate the order in which things come. *One, two,* and *three* (and all numbers ending in *one, two,* and *three,* except *eleven, twelve,* and *thirteen*) have irregular ordinals.

> *first, second, third*

All other ordinal numbers are formed by adding *-th.*

> *fourth, ninth, sixteenth*

Determiners

Determiners are often classified as adjectives (see page 16).

English Other adjectival forms

Many other kinds of words—even though they are not adjectives themselves—may be used as adjectives (that is, to describe a noun or pronoun).

NOUN	a ***philosophy*** *professor*
PRESENT PARTICIPLE	***running*** *water*
PAST PARTICIPLE	*the **required** reading*
PREPOSITIONAL PHRASE	*the poster **on the wall***
RELATIVE CLAUSE	*the poster **that I bought***
INFINITIVE	*I wondered what **to do**.*
ADVERBIAL PHRASE	*People **from all around** love him.*

spanish Other limiting adjectives

Ordinal numbers

In Spanish, ordinal numbers are essentially vocabulary items and must be learned as such. They agree in gender and number with the noun they modify.

>**primer** presidente
>**primera** actriz
>**quinto** tomo
>**décima** lección

Determiners

See pages 17–18.

spanish Other adjectival forms

NOUN PHRASE	*la sala **de conferencias***
PAST PARTICIPLE	*la tía **querida***
PREPOSITIONAL PHRASE	*reloj **de pared***
RELATIVE CLAUSE	*la ropa **que compré***
INFINITIVE	*No sé qué **hacer**.*
ADVERBIAL PHRASE	*Los estudiantes **en todas partes** sienten admiración por ella.*

Adverbs

Introducing adverbs

Definition   See page 7.

Forms   Most English adverbs formed from descriptive adjectives add *-ly* to the adjective.

> *active ~ active**ly***
> *slow ~ slow**ly***

1. Like adjectives, adverbs may be inflected to show comparison.

POSITIVE	COMPARATIVE	SUPERLATIVE
actively	*more actively*	*most actively*
actively	*less actively*	*least actively*

The comparative is used to show the similarity or difference between how two people or things do something, or the degree of difference in modifying an adjective or adverb. The superlative compares more than two people or things. There must also be a word to link the two points of comparison.

POSITIVE	*I walk **slowly**.*
COMPARATIVE	*John walks **more slowly than** I do.*
SUPERLATIVE	*Monica walks **the most slowly of** all.*

2. Like adjectives, some adverbs not ending in *-ly* may take *-er* and *-est* in comparisons.

> *He runs fast, but I run **faster**.*
> *Mary runs the **fastest** of all.*

3. Some adverbs form their comparison irregularly.

> *well ~ better ~ best*
> *badly ~ worse ~ worst*

CONTINUED ON PAGE 62 ▶

Spanish Introducing adverbs

Forms   Most Spanish adverbs formed from descriptive adjectives add *-mente* to the feminine form of the adjective. Most of these are adverbs of manner.

> *activa* (adjective) ~ **activamente** (adverb)
> *lenta* (adjective) ~ **lentamente** (adverb)

1. Like adjectives, adverbs may show comparison.

POSITIVE	COMPARATIVE	SUPERLATIVE
rápidamente	*más rápidamente*	*lo más rápidamente*
	tan rápidamente	
	menos rápidamente	*lo menos rápidamente*
naturalmente	*más naturalmente*	*lo más naturalmente*

The words used to link the two elements being compared are the same as for adjectives. (See **Quick Check** on page 49.)

POSITIVE	*Juan lee **rápidamente**.*
COMPARATIVE OF INEQUALITY	*Juan lee **más rápidamente que** Pedro.*
COMPARATIVE OF EQUALITY	*Marta lee **tan rápidamente como** Walter.*
SUPERLATIVE	*Rosita habla **lo más naturalmente**.*
SUPERLATIVE	*Consuelo lee **lo más rápidamente de** todos los estudiantes.*

Note that, unlike adjectives, the adverb has only one form.

2. Some of the most common adverbs do not end in *-mente* and must be learned as vocabulary items. They are compared, however, in the same way as *-mente* adverbs.

> *Juana llegó pronto; Juana llegó **tan pronto como** yo.*
> *Enrique se levanta temprano, pero Francisco se levanta **lo más temprano**.*

3. Four adverbs form their comparison irregularly.

POSITIVE	COMPARATIVE	SUPERLATIVE
bien ("well")	*mejor*	*mejor*
mal ("badly")	*peor*	*peor*
mucho	*más*	*más*
poco	*menos*	*menos*

Note that the comparative and superlative forms are identical.

4. When making a comparison of equality ("as much as") with verbs, use *tanto como* after the verb.

> *Francisco habla **tanto como** su padre.*   Francisco talks **as much as** his father does.

CONTINUED ON PAGE 63 ▶

Uses English adverbs are used in the following ways.

1. Adverbs answer the questions *how, when, where,* or *how much* about a verb, an adjective, or another adverb. Sometimes, a phrase takes the place of a single adverb.

> *Yesterday* he came **here** and **very**   **quickly** told the story.
> WHEN   WHERE   HOW MUCH HOW

> *This morning* he went **there**   **by car**.
> WHEN   WHERE HOW

2. **Negatives**. Some adverbs make a sentence negative. These include words like *not, nowhere,* and *never*. In standard English, two negative words in one sentence express a positive, not a negative, idea.

> *He doesn't have **no** friends, but he has **too few**.*

The first clause used alone and intended as a negative is not standard English. Not only are negative adverbs included here, but negative nouns and adjectives as well.

3. **Questions**. Another group of adverbs introduces questions: *when? where? how?* and *why?* The majority of adverbs answer these questions with respect to the verb, but the interrogative words themselves are adverbs too.

> ***When** does he arrive?*
> ***How** do you know that?*

4. **Relative clauses**. The same adverbs that ask questions may also be used to form relative clauses. These clauses tell when, where, how, or why the verb's action takes place and can be used in the same way.

> *We are going to the movies **when** we finish our work.*

Adjectives vs. adverbs

To choose the correct word, it is essential to ask yourself the following questions.

1. Am I *describing someone/something*? → adjective

2. Am I *describing how/when/where/why something is done*? → adverb

> *The **poem** is **good**, and the poet **reads** it **well**.*
> NOUN   ADJECTIVE   VERB   ADVERB

> *The **play** is **bad**, and it's **badly**   **performed**.*
> NOUN ADJECTIVE   ADVERB   VERB

This is especially important for verbs of mental or emotional state and for sensory verbs, which can be followed by either an adjective or an adverb. One of the most common examples is the following.

> *I feel **bad**.* (= I am sick/unhappy/etc.)
> *I feel **badly**.* (= My hands are not sensitive.)

Uses   Spanish adverbs are used in the following ways.

1. See the English on the opposite page.

   Ayer *vino* ***aquí*** *y* ***muy***   ***pronto*** *nos relató lo que pasó.*
   WHEN   WHERE   HOW MUCH   HOW

2. **Negatives.** In Spanish, the negative word *no* is an adverb and comes before

   a. a single verb.

      No hablo inglés.

   b. *haber, estar,* and *ser* when they are used in compound verb forms.

      No he visto a la maestra.
      No estamos trabajando mucho.
      El ladrón no fue capturado.

   c. object pronouns that precede verbs.

      No me gusta eso.

   Other common negative adverbs that accompany verbs are the following.

no... jamás	never	*no... nada*	not at all
no... nunca	never	*no... nadie*	no one
no... más	no longer	*no... ni... ni*	neither . . . nor

   Jamás, nunca, nada, and *nadie* can come either before or after the verb. If one of these negative adverbs follows the verb, *no* must precede the verb.

Nadie *me ama.* OR ***No*** *me ama* ***nadie.***	No one loves me.
Nunca *hablo inglés en México.*	I never speak English in Mexico.
OR ***No*** *hablo* ***nunca*** *inglés en México.*	
No *tengo* ***ni*** *tiempo* ***ni*** *dinero.*	I have neither time nor money.
No *hablo* ***ni*** *a Juan* ***ni*** *a Pedro.*	I speak neither to John nor to Peter.
No *leo* ***ni*** *hablo japonés.*	I neither read nor speak Japanese.
No *tengo ese libro* ***ni*** *puedo comprarlo.*	I don't have that book, nor can I buy it.

   Several negatives can be used in a single Spanish sentence—which you can't do in standard English.

*¡No! ¡**No** digo **nunca** **nada** a **nadie**!*	No! I never say anything to anyone!

3. **Questions (Interrogative adverbs)**

   *¿**Cuándo** llegaste? Llegué ayer.*
   *¿**Dónde** están los libros? Están en la mesa.*
   *¿**Cómo** te llamas? Me llamo Aldo.*

4. **Relative clauses**

   *Me acuesto **cuando termino mi trabajo.*** (The clause answers the question "when?")

Adjectives vs. adverbs

*El **poema** es **bueno** y el poeta lo **lee   bien.***
   NOUN   ADJECTIVE   VERB ADVERB

*La **obra** es **mala** y   se representa **mal.***
   NOUN   ADJECTIVE VERB   ADVERB

7

Conjunctions

English Introducing conjunctions

Definition   See page 7.

Forms   Conjunctions are function words; they are invariable.

Types   All conjunctions are linking words, but the linked elements and their relationship with each other determine which of the three principal types a conjunction belongs to: coordinating, subordinating, or adverbial.

Uses   English conjunctions are used as follows.

1. A **coordinating conjunction** links two equal elements that have the same grammatical construction. The two elements may be single words, phrases, or entire clauses.

NOUNS	*John **and** Mary*
INFINITIVES	*to be **or** not to be*
INDEPENDENT CLAUSES	*We came, **but** he was not there.*

Correlatives, which occur in pairs, are a subgroup of coordinating conjunctions.

***Both** John **and** Mary are in the class.*

2. A **subordinating conjunction** joins unequal elements. One element is subordinated to the other. The conjunction introduces the subordinate clause (the one that cannot stand alone as a sentence).

CONTRAST	***Although** he is hurrying, he is late.*
TIME	*We speak Spanish **when** the Rodríguez are here.*
CAUSE	***Because** this course is easy, we all get "A"s.*

Notice that the main idea of the sentence is in the main (independent) clause. The subordinate clause tells about the time, way, cause, or conditions involved and may show a contrast. Notice also that the main clause need not come first. You could reverse the order of the clauses in each example above without changing the meaning of the sentence.

There is also a subgroup of correlative subordinating conjunctions (for example, *if . . . then* and *so . . . that*).

*That course is **so hard that** many students fail.*

3. An **adverbial conjunction** is sometimes called a "conjunctive adverb." Grammarians are not sure whether they are really adverbs or conjunctions. Words and phrases like *therefore, perhaps, also, for example, as a result,* and *in other words* fall into this category.

spanish Introducing conjunctions

Uses Spanish conjunctions are used as follows.

1. Coordinating conjunctions

NOUNS	*Juan **y** María*
NOUNS	*Fernando **e** Isabel*
NOUNS	*septiembre **u** octubre*
INFINITIVES	*vivir **o** morir*
INDEPENDENT CLAUSES	*Vinimos para verlo, **pero** no estuvo en casa.*

Note that the conjunction *y* changes to *e* before another word beginning with an "ee" sound (spelled *i-* or *hi-*); the conjunction *o* changes to *u* before another "oh" sound.

Correlative conjunctions are a subgroup of coordinating conjunctions.

y... además	*Ella es bonita **y** fuerte **además**.*
ni... ni	*No tenemos **ni** tiempo **ni** dinero.*
o... o	***O** nos vamos ahora **o** no vamos nunca.*

2. Subordinating conjunctions

CONTRAST	***Aunque** se dio prisa, no llegó a tiempo.*
TIME	*Hablamos español **cuando** los Rodríguez están aquí.*
CAUSE	*Somos ricos **porque** mis padres siempre han trabajado duro.*

Correlative subordinates are a subgroup of subordinating conjunctions.

*Este curso es **tan** difícil **que** muchos estudiantes se quejan de él.*

3. Adverbial conjunctions

a menos que
dado que
desde que
excepto que
hasta que
mientras que
etc.

8

Interjections

English Introducing interjections

Definition   See page 7.

Forms   Interjections are normally invariable exclamations.

Uses   As an exclamation, an interjection is often merely a sound meant to convey emotion (for example, *ow!*). It has no grammatical connection with the other words in the sentence and is set off by commas.

Introducing interjections

Spanish interjections are simply vocabulary items that express exclamations. In Spanish, they are preceded by the inverted exclamation point (¡) and followed, as in English, by a standard exclamation point (!). Following are some common interjections in Spanish.

> ¡Alto!
> ¡Anda!
> ¡Ay!
> ¡Caramba!
> ¡Caray!
> ¡Cielos!
> ¡Cuidado!
> ¡Dios mío!
> ¡Dios!
> ¡Hola!
> ¡Huj!
> ¡Olé!

¡Qué! is also used in Spanish as an exclamation and translates as the English expression "What a _____!" or just "What _____!"

¡**Qué** niña más bonita!	What a pretty girl!
¡**Qué** alegría!	What joy!

9

Prepositions

Prepositions in any language are very tricky words. Most of them have basic meanings, but when they are used in phrasal verb constructions, that meaning can change. A phrasal verb is a combination of a verb plus (usually) a preposition that has a meaning different from the combined meanings of the words. You may think, for example, that you know what *up* means, but consider the following sentence.

> *First he cut the tree **down**, then he cut it **up**.*

People learning English would be confused by that sentence, and it is not an isolated example. Take the case of a friend telephoning John's house early in the morning and asking for him. John's wife might reply as follows.

> *He'll be **down** as soon as he's **up**.*

In other words, after learning a preposition and its basic meanings, one must be alert to how it is used in phrasal verb constructions. Often, the meanings of a single preposition will spread over several pages of a dictionary.

Definition   See page 7.

Forms   A preposition is a function word; it is invariable. It can be a single word or a group of words (for example, *by* and *in spite of*).

Uses   A preposition links a noun or pronoun (its object) to other words in the sentence and shows its relationship to them. In formal English, a preposition is followed immediately by its object.

> ***to** the store*
> ***about** the subject*

In informal English, a preposition is often placed at the end of the clause or sentence, especially in questions and relative clauses.

> ***What** is she waiting **for**?*
>   INSTEAD OF ***For what** is she waiting?*
> *This is the one **that** he is referring **to**.*
>   INSTEAD OF *This is the one **to which** he is referring.*

Forms   A Spanish preposition can be one or several words, for example, *en* ("in," "on") and *al lado de* ("beside," "next to").

Spanish prepositions are invariable, except for *a* and *de* (the two most common Spanish prepositions), which combine with the definite article *el* to form *al* and *del*.

> *Voy **al** cine.*
> *Es el libro **del** profesor.*
> *Vengo **del** mercado.*
> BUT
> *Vengo **a la** casa **de la** profesora.*

This contraction takes place even if *a* or *de* is part of a longer expression.

frente a	*frente **al** museo*	opposite the museum
enfrente de	*en frente **del** edificio*	in front of the building

Al + infinitive translates as English "upon" + gerund.

> *al hacer*   upon doing

Never expect a one-to-one equivalence between English and Spanish prepositions. They are capricious in both languages.

Uses   1. In English, many verbs are followed by prepositions that change the meaning of the verb. In Spanish, those different meanings are likely to be expressed by separate verbs.

buscar	to look **for**
mirar	to look **at**
investigar	to look **into**

2. English verbs are sometimes followed by a preposition that has an object, but not by a preposition alone. In Spanish, such verbs are never followed by a preposition.

> ENGLISH   Listen **to** the radio! Listen **to** it! BUT Listen!
> SPANISH   *¡Escuche la radio! ¡Escúchela!* AND *¡Escuche!*

3. In English, a preposition comes before its object in formal speech and writing, but it often appears at the end of a clause or sentence in informal English. In Spanish (and many other languages), a preposition must always be placed before its object.

> *¿**Con** quién vas al cine?*
>   (formal or informal Spanish)

> **With** whom are you going to the movies? (formal English)
> Who are you going to the movies **with**? (informal English)

4. An English preposition may be translated by more than one Spanish word. For example, in order to know how to say "before" in Spanish, you would need to know

   a. if it is a conjunction followed by a subject and verb (as in "**before** someone did something"). In this case, use *antes de que*.

   b. if it is a preposition expressing location (as in "**before** the door"). In this case, use *delante de*.

   c. if it is a preposition expressing time (as in "**before** 3 o'clock"). In this case, use *antes de*.

CONTINUED ON PAGE 76 ▶

Special problems with prepositions

1. For the uses of *para* and *por* meaning "for," see Appendix B.

2. Be sure to distinguish between prepositions that are expressed by the same word in English.

debajo de	under, underneath	*bajo de*	under (*figuratively*)
sobre	on	*encima de*	on (top of)

3. Verbs are often followed by infinitives. If two verbs are used to express a single thought, the first verb determines which preposition (if any) is used to introduce the infinitive that follows.

   Following is a list of common verbs and the prepositions they take when followed by an infinitive.

   aprender a to learn to
   > Yo **aprendí a** *conducir el coche este verano.*

   I **learned to** drive the car this summer.

   comenzar a to begin to
   > *La joven* **comenzó a** *reír.*

   The young woman **began to** laugh.

   enseñar a to teach to
   > *El profesor me* **enseñó a** *traducir bien el francés.*

   My teacher **taught** me **to** translate French well.

   enviar a to send to
   > *Mi madre me* **envió a** *comprar unos vegetales.*

   My mother **sent** me **to** buy some vegetables.

   ir a to go to
   > **Voy a** *verlo mañana.*

   I**'m going to** see him tomorrow.

   llegar a to come to, succeed in
   > **Llegué a** *aprender a hablar portugués.*

   I **succeeded in** learning to speak Portuguese.

   ponerse a to begin to
   > **Me puse a** *llorar.*

   I **started to** cry.

   tratar de to try to
   > **Trato de** *comenzar a leer este libro.*

   I**'m trying to** begin to read this book.

   venir a to come to
   > **Vengo a** *verlo mañana.*

   I**'m coming to** see him tomorrow.

   There can even be multiple infinitives in a string. In every case, if a verb is followed by an infinitive, the first of the two verbs determines the preposition.

Voy a tratar de comenzar a *leer este libro.*	I**'m going to try to begin to** read this book.
Quiero tratar de comenzar a *leer este libro.*	I **want to try to begin to** read this book.

   Note that in idiomatic expressions, the English preposition may or may not be the equivalent of the Spanish preposition.

CONTINUED ON PAGE 77 ▶

4. Some verbs require a specific preposition before a noun or pronoun object. These combinations must be memorized. Following are some common ones.

acabar con to put an end to
    Acabé con *la disputa.*   I **put an end to** the dispute.

acabar de to have just
    Él ***acaba de*** *verlos.*   He **has just** seen them.

acabar por to end up (finally)
    Enrique ***acabó por*** *darnos razón.*   Henry **finally** agreed with us.

dar a to face toward, look out on
    La ventana ***da a*** *la plaza.*   The window **looks out on** the square.

felicitarse de to congratulate oneself on
    Se felicitaron de *ganar el premio.*   They **congratulated themselves on** winning the prize.

mirar por to look out of, look through
    Miré por *la ventana.*   I **looked out of** the window.

ocuparse en to be busy with
    Nos ocupamos en *nuestros estudios.*   We **are busy with** our studies.

reírse de to laugh at
    Se rio de *mí.*   He **laughed at** me.

5. Some adjectives are followed by a preposition before an infinitive, just as some verbs are. Spanish and English often use different prepositions.

último/última en
    Manuela es siempre la ***última en*** *terminar.*   Manuela is always the **last one to** finish.

lento/lenta en
    Yo soy muy ***lento en*** *aprender la química.*   I'm very **slow at** learning chemistry.

necesario/necesaria para
    La física es ***necesaria para*** *comprender el universo.*   Physics is **necessary for** learning about the universe.

listo/lista para
    Yo estoy ***lista para*** *la llegada de mis padres.*   I'm **ready for** my parents' arrival.

10

Verbs

Introducing verbs

Definition See page 7.

Forms English has fewer inflected verb forms than any continental European language. Many English verbs have only four forms (for example, *talk, talks, talked, talking*); some have five forms (for example, *sing, sings, sang, sung, singing*).

In some systems of grammar, it is said that, technically, English has only two tenses—present and past—and that other temporal concepts are expressed by periphrastic verbal constructions. This means that English uses helping verbs and other expressions to convey temporal differences. Verbs are presented here in a more traditional way, because it will help you see the parallels between English and Spanish constructions. Following are the principal parts of an English verb.

INFINITIVE	SIMPLE PAST	PAST PARTICIPLE	PRESENT PARTICIPLE
talk	*talked*	*talked*	*talking*
sing	*sang*	*sung*	*singing*

Some words used to identify verb forms are **conjugation**, **tense**, **voice**, **transitive**, **intransitive**, and **mood**.

Conjugation

This word has two meanings.

1. In Latin and in modern Romance languages, verbs are classified into groups, or conjugations, by their infinitive endings. English and German have only *regular* and *irregular* (sometimes called *weak* and *strong*) verbs. Weak verbs take a regular ending to form the past (for example, *talk ~ talked* and *follow ~ followed*). Strong verbs often change the vowel in their past forms and may look completely different from the infinitive (for example, *sing ~ sang* and *go ~ went*).

2. Conjugation also refers to a list, by person, of each form in a given tense. Latin has six forms in each tense. Following are the present-tense forms of *amare* ("to love").

	SINGULAR	PLURAL
FIRST PERSON	*amo* I love	*amamus* we love
SECOND PERSON	*amas* you (singular) love	*amatis* you (plural) love
THIRD PERSON	*amat* he/she loves	*amant* they love

Since each form is different, it is not necessary to use a pronoun subject: The verb ending tells you who the subject is. The same is true for Spanish today.

In English, verbs can be conjugated but usually are not, because there is only one inflected ending: *-s* is added to the third-person singular of the simple present tense.

	SINGULAR	PLURAL
FIRST PERSON	*I speak*	*we speak*
SECOND PERSON	*you speak*	*you speak*
THIRD PERSON	*he/she speaks*	*they speak*

The pronoun (or a noun) is required with every verb form, because otherwise it would not be known who or what the subject is.

Tense

This word comes from Latin *tempus* via French *temps*, meaning "time." The tense tells *when* something happened, *how long* it lasted, and whether it is *completed*.

Voice

English has two voices: active and passive. **Active voice** means that the subject is or is doing something.

> *Mary is happy.*
> *Mary reads the newspaper.*

In these examples, *Mary* is the subject.

Passive voice means that the subject is acted on by an agent. The verb tells what happens to the subject.

> *The newspaper is read by Mary.*

In this example, *newspaper* is the subject.

Transitive verbs

These verbs require an object to express a complete meaning.

> *Mr. White surprised a burglar.*

In this example, the verb *surprised* is transitive, because it takes an object, *burglar*. If we omitted the object, the sentence would not make sense; it would be incomplete.

Intransitive verbs

These verbs do not require an object.

> *Paul sat down.*

Here, the verb *sat* is intransitive, because it has no object; *down* is an adverb.

English has many verbs that can be either transitive or intransitive.

Peter	***eats***	*dinner*	*at 7 o'clock.*
The butcher	***weighs***	*the meat.*	
SUBJECT	TRANSITIVE VERB	DIRECT OBJECT	

Peter	***eats***	*at 7 o'clock.*
The butcher	***weighs***	*a lot.*
SUBJECT	INTRANSITIVE VERB	

Mood

This grammatical concept indicates the mood, or attitude, of the speaker. Is the speaker stating a fact? Offering a possibility that has not happened yet? Making a recommendation? Giving an order? Three moods are used to express these ideas: indicative, imperative, and subjunctive. The indicative is by far the most common mood. The other two are used in special circumstances and are discussed below.

English Introducing questions

Forms   There are four ways to ask a question in English.

1. Place a question mark after a statement and raise the pitch of your voice at the end of the statement when saying it aloud.

    Anne is here already?
    That's Mark's idea?

2. Add a "tag," repeating the verb or auxiliary verb as a negative question. In English, the specific tag depends on the subject and the verb.

    *Peter is happy, **isn't he**?*
    *They came on time, **didn't they**?*

3. Invert the subject and an auxiliary or modal verb or the verb *to be*.

PRESENT	***Do you*** *have any brothers?*
PRESENT PROGRESSIVE	***Is Peter*** *buying his books?*
PRESENT	***Does Peter*** *buy his books?*
PRESENT PERFECT	***Has Peter*** *bought his books?*
PRESENT	***May I*** *see you this evening?*
PRESENT	***Is Robert*** *here today?*

4. Use an interrogative word.

    Where *is the library?*
    When *does the library open?*

Forms In Spanish, there are six ways to ask a question when using the simple tenses (one-word verb forms).

1. Place question marks before and after a statement, and raise the pitch of your voice at the end of the statement when saying it aloud. This method is usually limited to conversations (oral and written).

   > ¿Ana está aquí ya?

2. Place ¿no es verdad?, ¿verdad?, or ¿no? after a statement with which you expect the hearer or reader to agree.

   > Pedro está muy contento, ¿no es verdad?
   > Tienes dinero, ¿no?

3. Invert the subject noun or pronoun and the verb when no object noun or adverb is present. You do not need an auxiliary verb to form a question, as you do in English.

   > ¿Trabaja Juan?
   > ¿Estudian ustedes?

4. Place the subject noun after the verb's object noun, adverb (if present), or adjective (if it follows ser or estar).

   > ¿Toca el piano Miguel?
   > ¿Canta bien Pablo?
   > ¿Era bonita la niña?

5. Place the subject pronoun immediately after the verb when an object noun or pronoun is present.

   > ¿Habla usted portugués?

6. Begin the sentence with an interrogative word.

   > ¿Dónde está María?
   > ¿A qué hora se abre la biblioteca?

When using compound tenses (multiple-word verb forms), place the verb in front of the subject.

   > ¿Ha visto usted a Juan?
   > ¿Está cantando Luisa en Nueva York o en Los Ángeles?
   > ¿A qué hora habría llegado usted si no hubiera un tren?

However, note the difference in the placement of the subject pronoun in the first example below and the placement of the subject noun in the second one.

   > ¿Ha estado usted estudiando todos los días?
   > ¿Han estado estudiando los estudiantes todos los días?

Introducing verbals

Definition Verbals are forms of the verb that are not finite, that is, do not agree with a subject and do not function as the predicate of a sentence. There are five types of verbals: present infinitive, past infinitive, gerund, present participle (also called the gerundive), and past participle.

English Present infinitives

Definition The present infinitive is the basic form of the verb, as it appears in a dictionary.

Forms The infinitive is often identified by the word *to* preceding it. However, *to* is omitted in many infinitive constructions, especially after verbs like *can* and *let*. Compare the following sentences, both of which contain the infinitive *swim*.

> *I know how **to swim**.*
> *I can **swim**.*

Uses In addition to completing the verb, as in the above examples, an infinitive may serve as the subject or object of a sentence, as an adjective, or as an adverb.

> SUBJECT   ***To err** is human.*
> OBJECT   *He hopes **to come** soon.*
> ADJECTIVE   *English is the subject **to study**.*
> ADVERB   ***To tell the truth**, he wants it more than ever.*

Infinitives may also have their own direct objects and other modifiers.

> *I am able **to do** that   easily.*
>   DIRECT OBJECT ADVERB

English Past infinitives

Forms The past infinitive is formed with the present infinitive of the auxiliary verb plus the past participle of the main verb.

> *to go* (present infinitive) → *to have gone* (past infinitive)

Uses The past infinitive is used in the same ways as the present infinitive.

> ***To have quit** is terrible.*

Spanish Present infinitives

Forms   Spanish verbs are grouped in three conjugations according to the ending of their infinitives: *-ar* (the most common), *-er*, and *-ir*.

Uses   The Spanish infinitive may be used in several ways.

SUBJECT/COMPLEMENT	*Ver es creer.*
OBJECT	*Raúl espera llegar pronto.*
OBJECT OF A PREPOSITION	*Voy a decírselo a tu padre.*
ADJECTIVE	*El inglés es una lengua para estudiar.*
ADVERB	*A decir verdad, no lo creo yo.*

Infinitives may have objects (either nouns or pronouns) and be negated or otherwise modified.

Voy a ver el museo.
Quiero comprender mejor la filosofía.
Voy a mostrárselo a la señora García.
Prefiero no llegar a tiempo.

An infinitive may have both a direct and an indirect object.

Voy a leerle el periódico al señor Robles.
Voy a leérselo.

Remember that *le* and *les* become *se* when used before *lo, la, los,* or *las.*

Spanish Past infinitives

Forms   Past infinitives are formed as in English, with the present infinitive of the auxiliary *haber* plus the past participle of the main verb.

PRESENT INFINITIVE	PAST INFINITIVE
estudiar	*haber estudiado*
vender	*haber vendido*
escribir	*haber escrito*

Uses   The past infinitive may be used in the same ways as the present infinitive, but with an element of expressing past time.

Quería haber escrito una novela antes de morir.	He wanted to have written a novel before dying.

 Gerunds

Definition Gerunds are often called verbal nouns.

Forms The English gerund is formed by adding *-ing* to the infinitive form of the verb.

sing → singing
run → running
bite → biting

Uses Gerunds have the same functions as other nouns (see page 10).

SUBJECT ***Walking*** *is good for you.*
OBJECT *I like* ***singing***.

Gerunds may also have objects and modifiers.

Making *money   quickly is many people's goal.*
       DIRECT OBJECT ADVERB

English Participles

Definition Participles are verbal adjectives that constitute the third and fourth principal parts of a verb.

Forms English has two participles.

1. **Present participles** (the fourth principal part) end in *-ing.*

   singing
   talking
   managing

2. **Past participles** (the third principal part) end in *-ed* or *-n* for regular verbs.

   tried
   gathered
   concentrated
   given

   To determine the past participle of an irregular verb, say, "Today I go; yesterday I went; I have gone; I am going." The form used after "I have" is the past participle. In the dictionary, the principal parts are given for every irregular verb.

Uses The two types of participles have the same basic uses.

1. As part of a compound verb (one consisting of two or more words)

   PRESENT PROGRESSIVE *He* ***is talking***.
   PAST PERFECT *They* ***have given***.

2. As an adjective

   a ***talking*** *doll*
   a ***proven*** *fact*

3. In an absolute phrase modifying a noun

   Walking *along the street, he met Robin.*
   Seen *from the front, the building was even more imposing.*

   In the two examples above, *he* is *walking* and *the building* was *seen.*

Spanish Gerunds

Spanish has no gerund; the infinitive is used as the verbal noun (see page 85, the subject/complement example under Present infinitives). Infinitives may be modified.

Ganar dinero rápidamente es el objetivo de muchas personas.

Spanish Participles

Forms Spanish has two participles.

1. **Present participles** are invariable, that is, they do not change for gender or number.

    The Spanish present participle is formed as follows.

STEM	Drop the *-ar, -er,* or *-ir* infinitive ending.
ENDINGS	Add *-ando* to the stem of *-ar* verbs and *-iendo* to the stem of *-er* and *-ir* verbs.

hablar	habl**ando**
aprender	aprend**iendo**
vivir	viv**iendo**

    -Ir stem-changing verbs change *e* to *i* and *o* to *u* in the stem of the present participle.

sentir	sintiendo
pedir	pidiendo
dormir	durmiendo

    The following verbs and their compounds (verbs formed by adding a prefix to the basic verb) change the *i* of *-iendo* ending to *y*. Included in this group are verbs ending in *-uir* or *-üir* (except those ending in *-guir*).

caer	cayendo
destruir	destruyendo
traer	trayendo
creer	creyendo
ir	yendo
oír	oyendo

    Some common verbs have irregular present participles.

venir	viniendo
decir	diciendo
poder	pudiendo

CONTINUED ON PAGE 88 ▶

Verbs ending in *-eír*, like *reír* ("to laugh") and *sonreír* ("to smile"), eliminate both the *e* and the written accent when forming the present participle.

reír	**riendo**
sonreír	*sonriendo*

2. **Past participles** are typically formed by dropping the *-ar*, *-er*, or *-ir* ending from the infinitive and adding *-ado* to *-ar* verbs and *-ido* to *-er* and *-ir* verbs.

hablar	*habl**ado***
vender	*vend**ido***
pedir	*ped**ido***

A number of Spanish verbs have irregular past participles; following are some of the most common.

abrir	*abierto*
cubrir	*cubierto*
decir	*dicho*
escribir	*escrito*
hacer	*hecho*
morir	*muerto*
poner	*puesto*
romper	*roto*
soltar	*suelto*
ver	*visto*
volver	*vuelto*

A compound verb normally forms its past participle in the same way as the basic verb: *deponer*, **depuesto**; *describir*, **descrito**; *entreabrir*, **entreabierto**; *revolver*, **revuelto**.

Uses   A **present participle** is used

1. with forms of *estar* to form the progressive tenses.

> *María **está cantando**.*
> *Juan **estaba explicando**.*

2. after the verbs *continuar* and *seguir* in place of an infinitive.

> *Julio **continúa aprendiendo** inglés.*
> *Ana **siguió leyendo**.*

3. in a subordinate clause when its subject is the same as that of the main clause.

> ***Conociendo** muy bien la ciudad, Elena dio un paseo.*

Be sure that the participle modifies the correct noun, so that you avoid a dangling participial phrase (such as "I saw the church, walking up the hill"—who or what is walking?). Place the noun or pronoun to be modified next to the participial phrase.

Some nouns and adjectives have endings that resemble a present participle and were once verbals. This may help you to guess or remember their meanings.

la vivienda	housing
la hacienda	ranch, fortune
siguiente	following
ambulante	walking

CONTINUED ON PAGE 89 ▶

A past participle is used

1. with forms of *haber* to form the perfect tenses.

   *Eduardo **ha terminado** su trabajo.*
   *Eduardo **había terminado** su trabajo.*

2. as an adjective.

   *el libro **abierto***
   *la Tierra **Prometida***
   *el Mar **Muerto***

3. as a noun.

   *el Valle de los **Caídos***

Indicative mood

The verbs on pages 90–113 are all in the indicative mood. It is the one used for stating facts and for making assertions as though they were facts.

English Present tenses

Definition   The present tense is defined by its uses (see below).

Forms   There are three present tenses in English: simple present, present progressive, and present emphatic.

1. **Simple present**. There is only one inflected form in the simple present: the third-person singular, which adds *-s* to the basic verb form.

	SINGULAR	PLURAL
FIRST PERSON	*I sing*	*we sing*
SECOND PERSON	*you sing*	*you sing*
THIRD PERSON	*he/she sings*	*they sing*

2. **Present progressive**. This tense is formed with the present tense of *to be* plus the present participle.

	SINGULAR	PLURAL
FIRST PERSON	*I am singing*	*we are singing*
SECOND PERSON	*you are singing*	*you are singing*
THIRD PERSON	*he/she is singing*	*they are singing*

3. **Present emphatic**. This tense is formed with the present tense of *to do* plus the infinitive.

	SINGULAR	PLURAL
FIRST PERSON	*I do sing*	*we do sing*
SECOND PERSON	*you do sing*	*you do sing*
THIRD PERSON	*he/she does sing*	*they do sing*

CONTINUED ON PAGE 92 ▶

spanish Present tense

Forms   The Spanish present tense includes two tenses: the simple present and the present progressive. The simple present form *hablo* may be translated as "I speak," "I am speaking," and "I do speak." The present progressive is used only if you wish to stress the fact the action is going on now: *estoy hablando* ("I am speaking").

1. **Regular -*ar* verbs**. Drop the -*ar* and add -*a, -as, -a; -amos, -áis, -an*.

    hablar

	SINGULAR	PLURAL
FIRST PERSON	hablo	hablamos
SECOND PERSON	hablas	habláis
THIRD PERSON	habla	hablan

    The present progressive tense uses the present tense of *estar* and the present participle ending in -*ando*, as shown in the chart that follows.

	SINGULAR	PLURAL
FIRST PERSON	estoy hablando	estamos hablando
SECOND PERSON	estás hablando	estáis hablando
THIRD PERSON	está hablando	están hablando

    The verbs *ser, estar, ir,* and *venir* are never used in the progressive tenses as the main verb.

2. **Regular -*er* verbs**. Drop the -*er* and add -*o, -es, -e; -emos, -éis, -en*.

    aprender

	SINGULAR	PLURAL
FIRST PERSON	aprendo	aprendemos
SECOND PERSON	aprendes	aprendéis
THIRD PERSON	aprende	aprenden

    The present progressive tense uses the present tense of *estar* and the present participle ending in -*iendo*, as in *estoy aprendiendo*.

3. **Regular -*ir* verbs**. Drop the -*ir* and add -*o, -es, -e; -imos, -ís, -en*.

    vivir

	SINGULAR	PLURAL
FIRST PERSON	vivo	vivimos
SECOND PERSON	vives	vivís
THIRD PERSON	vive	viven

    The present progressive tense uses the present tense of *estar* and the present participle ending in -*iendo*, as in *estoy viviendo*.

CONTINUED ON PAGE 92 ▶

Uses   The **simple present** is used for

1. an action or state occurring in the present.

    *They **speak** Chinese.*

2. an habitual action that is still true.

    *I always **study** in the evening.*

3. existing facts and eternal truths.

    *Madrid **is** the capital of Spain.*
    *Time **is** money.*

The **present progressive** is used to

1. stress the continuing nature of the verb's action in either a statement or a question.

    *I **am** still **trying**!*
    ***Are** you **going** to the library now?*

2. make a future action seem more immediate.

    *We **are reading** this book next week.*
    *I **am going** to the show tomorrow.*

The **present emphatic** is used to

1. add emphasis or contradict.

    *I **do want** to do well.*
    *They **do** not **do** that!*

2. form questions or negative statements.

    ***Do** you **go** to the lake in the summer?*
    *I **do** not **know** what you are talking about.*

Spanish   Present tense (continued)

4. **Stem-changing verbs.** Changes in the stem of a conjugated verb occur as the result of a change in stress in the oral language.

    a. *-ar* verbs

    In *-ar* verbs, *e → ie* and *o → ue* in all forms except the *nosotros* and *vosotros* forms. *Jugar* is unusual in that *u → ue*.

pensar	*e → ie*	*pienso*	BUT	*pensamos, pensáis*
mostrar	*o → ue*	*muestras*	BUT	*mostramos, mostráis*
jugar	*u → ue*	*juega*	BUT	*jugamos, jugáis*

    b. *-er* and *-ir* verbs

    In *-er* and *-ir* verbs, *e → ie* and *o → ue* in all forms except the *nosotros* and *vosotros* forms.

entender	*e → ie*	*entiendo*	BUT	*entendemos, entendéis*
volver	*o → ue*	*vuelves*	BUT	*volvemos, volvéis*
sentir	*e → ie*	*siento*	BUT	*sentimos, sentís*
dormir	*o → ue*	*duermes*	BUT	*dormimos, dormís*

CONTINUED ON PAGE 93 ▶

In certain *-ir* verbs, *e → i* in all forms except the *nosotros* and *vosotros* forms.

pedir   *e → i*   *pido*   BUT *pedimos, pedís*

Other common verbs following this pattern are *repetir, seguir, servir,* and *vestir.*

5. **Orthographic (spelling) changing verbs.** Some verbs require a spelling change to preserve proper pronunciation in the present indicative.*

   a. In verbs ending in *-ger* (for example, *escoger*), *g* changes to *j* in the first-person singular: *escojo.* The *g* is retained in *escoges, escoge,* etc.

   b. In verbs ending in *-guir* (for example, *distinguir*), *gu* changes to *g* in the first-person singular: *distingo.* The *gu* is retained in *distingues, distingue,* etc.

   c. In verbs ending in a consonant plus *-cer* (for example, *vencer*), *c* changes to *z* in the first-person singular: *venzo.* The *c* is retained in *vences, vence,* etc.

   d. In verbs ending in a vowel plus *-cer* or *-cir* (for example, *conocer*), *c* changes to *zc* in the first-person singular: *conozco.* The *c* is retained in *conoces, conoce,* etc. (Other verbs like this include *ofrecer, parecer, producir,* and *traducir.*)

   e. In verbs ending in *-fiar* and *-viar* (for example, *confiar*), plus some verbs that end in a consonant plus *-uar* (for example, *continuar*), a written accent is required on the *i* or *u* in all written forms of the present indicative except the *nosotros* and *vosotros* forms.

   confiar: confío, confías, confía; confiamos, confiáis, confían
   enviar: envío, envías, envía; enviamos, enviáis, envían
   continuar: continúo, continúas, continúa; continuamos, continuáis, continúan
   conceptuar: conceptúo, conceptúas, conceptúa; conceptuamos, conceptuáis, conceptúan

6. The first-person singular of some verbs ends in *-oy.*

dar	*doy*	*ir*	*voy*
estar	*estoy*	*ser*	*soy*

7. The first-person singular of some verbs ends in *-go.*

decir	*digo*	*salir*	*salgo*
hacer	*hago*	*tener*	*tengo*
oír	*oigo*	*traer*	*traigo*
poner	*pongo*		

Uses

1. All of the uses listed for the three present tenses in English are filled by the simple present tense in Spanish. To emphasize that one is in the act of doing something, use the present progressive tense.

2. Spanish uses the present tense form *hace* (from *hacer*) + a time expression + *que* for an action begun in the past that is still going on in the present.

***Hace dos meses que** estudio español.*	I have been studying Spanish for two months. (I began studying Spanish two months ago, and I am still studying it.)

---

*In Spanish, *c* is pronounced *s* before *e* and *i,* as in the words *ciudad* and *centro*; before other vowels, the letter *c* has a *k* sound, as in the words *cámara, collar,* and *curva.* The letter *g* is pronounced *h* before *e* and *i,* as in the words *gente* and *giro*; before other vowels, the letter *g* has a hard *g* sound, as in the words *gafas, goma,* and *guacamole.*

English Past tenses

Definition The past tenses describe actions or states in the past.

Forms There are three past tenses, each corresponding to one of the three present tenses discussed in the previous section. (For perfect tenses, see pages 102–111.)

1. The **simple past** is the second principal part of the verb (see page 80). It is not inflected; all of the forms are the same. The simple past of weak verbs ends in *-ed* (for example, *talked* and *wished*). Strong verbs have irregular past forms.

	SINGULAR	PLURAL
FIRST PERSON	*I sang*	*we sang*
SECOND PERSON	*you sang*	*you sang*
THIRD PERSON	*he/she sang*	*they sang*

2. The **past progressive** is formed with the simple past of the verb *to be* plus the present participle of the main verb.

	SINGULAR	PLURAL
FIRST PERSON	*I was singing*	*we were singing*
SECOND PERSON	*you were singing*	*you were singing*
THIRD PERSON	*he/she was singing*	*they were singing*

3. The **past emphatic** is formed with the simple past of the verb *to do* plus the infinitive.

	SINGULAR	PLURAL
FIRST PERSON	*I did sing*	*we did sing*
SECOND PERSON	*you did sing*	*you did sing*
THIRD PERSON	*he/she did sing*	*they did sing*

Uses The three past tenses closely parallel the three present tenses in usage, except that the action takes place in the past. The simple past is a statement of a fact, the past progressive emphasizes the duration or continuation of an action at a given moment in the past, and the past emphatic stresses a statement and is used to form negatives and questions.

Other past forms

Other expressions provide special past meanings.

1. Immediate past action: *to have just* plus the past participle

    Mary **has just arrived** this minute.

2. Habitual past action: *used to* or *would* plus the infinitive

    I **used to go** to the movies every week.
    For a long time, I **would see** them every day.

3. Repeated past action: *kept (on)* plus the present participle

    He **kept (on) doing** it.

Imperfect tense

Forms
The imperfect tense of regular verbs is formed with the verb stem plus special endings. The stem is formed by dropping the *-ar*, *-er*, or *-ir* ending of the infinitive. Imperfect endings for *-ar* verbs are *-aba, -abas, -aba; -ábamos, -abais, -aban*. Imperfect endings for *-er* and *-ir* verbs are *-ía,- ías, -ía; -íamos, -íais, -ían*.

hablar	perder	salir
hablaba	perdía	salía
hablabas	perdías	salías
hablaba	perdía	salía
hablábamos	perdíamos	salíamos
hablabais	perdíais	salíais
hablaban	perdían	salían

Only three Spanish verbs are irregular in the imperfect: *ir, ser,* and *ver*. Note that it is only the stem that really presents a problem.

ir	iba, ibas, iba; íbamos, ibais, iban
ser	era, eras, era; éramos, erais, eran
ver	veía, veías, veía; veíamos, veíais, veían

The imperfect progressive is formed with the imperfect of *estar* plus the present participle.

hablar	perder	salir
estaba hablando	estaba perdiendo	estaba saliendo
estabas hablando	estabas perdiendo	estabas saliendo
estaba hablando	estaba perdiendo	estaba saliendo
estábamos hablando	estábamos perdiendo	estábamos saliendo
estabais hablando	estabais perdiendo	estabais saliendo
estaban hablando	estaban perdiendo	estaban saliendo

Uses
The Spanish imperfect tense is used for

1. description: What you are describing is more important than the action or is the background against which the action takes place. See the English "used to" construction.

2. habitual action: See the English "used to/would" construction.

3. duration or continuing action: See the English past progressive.

The imperfect tense is used on the basis of these principles, not on a one-to-one correspondence with English tenses or idioms. The imperfect is often used in Spanish when the simple past tense is used in English.

DESCRIPTION	***Era*** lunes y ***llovía***.	It was Monday, and it was raining.
HABITUAL ACTION/ DESCRIPTION	Yo ***asistía*** a Park Place School cuando ***era*** niña.	I went to Park Place School when I was a child.
DURATION	***Leía*** el periódico cuando sonó el teléfono.	He was reading the newspaper when the telephone rang.
	Isabel ***continuaba*** riéndose.	Isabel kept on laughing.

CONTINUED ON PAGE 96 ▶

Other past tenses

Other tenses used to describe past time are the preterite (see page 97), the present perfect (see pages 103 and 105), the present perfect progressive (see page 105), the past perfect (pluperfect) (see page 105), the preterite perfect (see page 107), the past perfect progressive (see page 107), the conditional perfect (see page 111), the conditional perfect progressive (see page 111), the imperfect subjunctive (see page 121), and the past perfect (pluperfect) subjunctive (see page 123).

The following chart contrasts the imperfect tense with the preterite tense, which is used for completed actions.

PRETERITE	IMPERFECT
Action happened one or more times	Action happened often (repeated/habitual)
Finished and completed action	Continuing, unfinished action
Series of distinct events	Description
María **terminó** *sus deberes.*	*María* **terminaba** *a menudo muy tarde.*
El teléfono **sonó**	*mientras que él* **dormía.**
Rodrigo **llegó** *a Asunción,* **halló** *un hotel y* **se quedó** *allá en Santa Fe.*	*Manolo* **era** *un estudiante mexicano que* **vivía** *en Texas pero que* **tomaba** *sus vacaciones en Chile.*

Other past forms

1. For the immediate past, use the present tense of *acabar de* plus an infinitive.

   María **acaba de llegar**.   Mary has just arrived.

2. To express "had just" plus a past participle in English, use the imperfect tense of *acabar de* plus the infinitive.

   Miguel **acababa de llegar**.   Michael had just arrived.

3. For "used to" or "would" plus infinitive, use the imperfect tense.

   Cuando yo **era** *joven, yo* **iba** *al cine todos los sábados por la tarde.*   When I was young, I used to go to the movies every Saturday afternoon.

Preterite tense

1. The preterite tense is formed with the verb stem plus special endings. Preterite endings for *-ar* verbs are *-é, -aste, -ó; -amos, -asteis, -aron.* Preterite endings for *-er* and *-ir* verbs are *-í, -iste, -ió; -imos, -isteis, -ieron.*

hablar	perder	salir
hablé	perdí	salí
hablaste	perdiste	saliste
habló	perdió	salió
hablamos	perdimos	salimos
hablasteis	perdisteis	salisteis
hablaron	perdieron	salieron

2. Several Spanish verbs have irregular preterite forms. Following are some of the most common.

andar	anduve, anduviste, anduvo; anduvimos, anduvisteis, anduvieron
caber	cupe, cupiste, cupo; cupimos, cupisteis, cupieron
dar	di, diste, dio; dimos, disteis, dieron
decir	dije, dijiste, dijo; dijimos, dijisteis, dijeron
dormir	dormí, dormiste, durmió; dormimos, dormisteis, durmieron
estar	estuve, estuviste, estuvo; estuvimos, estuvisteis, estuvieron
haber	hube, hubiste, hubo; hubimos, hubisteis, hubieron
hacer	hice, hiciste, hizo; hicimos, hicisteis, hicieron
ir	fui, fuiste, fue; fuimos, fuisteis, fueron
poder	pude, pudiste, pudo; pudimos, pudisteis, pudieron
poner	puse, pusiste, puso; pusimos, pusisteis, pusieron
querer	quise, quisiste, quiso; quisimos, quisisteis, quisieron
saber	supe, supiste, supo; supimos, supisteis, supieron
sentir	sentí, sentiste, sintió; sentimos, sentisteis, sintieron
ser	fui, fuiste, fue; fuimos, fuisteis, fueron
tener	tuve, tuviste, tuvo; tuvimos, tuvisteis, tuvieron
traducir	traduje, tradujiste, tradujo; tradujimos, tradujisteis, tradujeron
traer	traje, trajiste, trajo; trajimos, trajisteis, trajeron
venir	vine, viniste, vino; vinimos, vinisteis, vinieron

Verbs ending in *-car, -gar,* and *-zar* have orthographic (spelling) changes in the first-person singular (*yo*) form only.

buscar	bus**qué**
pagar	pa**gué**
empezar	empe**cé**

Verbs ending in *-ducir* follow the pattern of *traducir* above.

The preterite perfect is formed with the preterite of *haber* plus the past participle. It is a literary form and is used only after time expressions.

*Cuando Consuelo me **hubo hablado**, me di cuenta de que tenía razón.*   When Consuelo had spoken to me, I realized that she was right.

Uses The preterite in Spanish is roughly equivalent to the simple past in English. It tells about completed action in the past. See page 96 for uses of the preterite contrasted with those of the imperfect.

English Future tenses

Definition   Future tenses describe events that have not yet taken place.

Forms   There are only two tenses for future time: the future and the future progressive. Both are compound tenses, that is, they require more than one word to form them.

1. The **future tense** is formed by using the auxiliary verb *will* plus the infinitive of the main verb.

	SINGULAR	PLURAL
FIRST PERSON	*I will sing*	*we will sing*
SECOND PERSON	*you will sing*	*you will sing*
THIRD PERSON	*he/she will sing*	*they will sing*

2. The **future progressive tense** is formed with the future of *to be* plus the present participle. It therefore requires three words.

	SINGULAR	PLURAL
FIRST PERSON	*I will be singing*	*we will be singing*
SECOND PERSON	*you will be singing*	*you will be singing*
THIRD PERSON	*he/she will be singing*	*they will be singing*

NOTES

1. There are no irregular future tense forms in English.

2. *Will* is often contracted to *'ll*.

> *We'll do it tomorrow.*
> *You'll be studying that next week.*

Uses   The distinction between the future and future progressive tenses is the same as that between the corresponding tenses in the present tenses (see page 92). They are used

1. to express an action or state that will happen or exist in the future.

2. in Type 1 conditional sentences, where the *if*-clause is in the present. (See **Quick Check** on page 110.)

> *If you **study**, you **will succeed**.*

Other future forms

Another way to express future action is an idiomatic use of *to go* plus the infinitive of the main verb.

> *I **am going to sing** tomorrow.*

Future tense

Forms There is only one future tense in Spanish. It is formed with a stem plus special endings. The stem is the full infinitive, and the endings are -é, -ás, -á; -emos, -éis, -án.

1. Future stems always end in -r.

2. The endings are the same for all verbs, even irregular verbs. All irregularities are in the stem, so once you know the stem, you know all of the forms.

3. All of the endings except the *nosotros* form have a written accent.

hablar	perder	dormir	ser	estar
hablaré	perderé	dormiré	seré	estaré
hablarás	perderás	dormirás	serás	estarás
hablará	perderá	dormirá	será	estará
hablaremos	perderemos	dormiremos	seremos	estaremos
hablaréis	perderéis	dormiréis	seréis	estaréis
hablarán	perderán	dormirán	serán	estarán

A number of Spanish verbs have irregular stems in the future, even though their endings are regular. These stems are also used to form the conditional tense (see page 101).

caber	**cabr**é	salir	**saldr**é
haber	**habr**ás	tener	**tendr**ás
poder	**podr**á	valer	**valdr**á
querer	**querr**emos	venir	**vendr**emos
saber	**sabr**éis	decir	**dir**éis
poner	**podr**án	hacer	**har**án

Uses The future tense in Spanish is used

1. to express an action or state that will happen or exist.

   *Marco **llegará** en enero.*   Mark will arrive in January.

2. in Type 1 conditional sentences, where the *if*-clause is in the present. (See **Quick Check** on page 111.)

   *Si Uds. **estudian**, Uds. **saldrán** bien.*   If you study, you will succeed.

3. as a command for the future.

   ***Presentarán** sus estudios el miércoles.*   You will give your reports on Wednesday.

   *No **matarás**.*   Thou shalt not kill.

4. to indicate possibility.

   *¿Quién **será**? **Será** tu hermano.*   I wonder who that is? It must be your brother.

   *¿**Será** posible?*   Is it possible?

Other future forms

Like "to go" plus an infinitive in English, the present tense of *ir* + *a* + the infinitive of the main verb can express future time or intention in Spanish.

   ***Voy a cantar** mañana.*   I am going to sing tomorrow.

Definition Many grammarians do not consider the conditional to be a true tense, but rather a mood. We consider it a tense here, however, since this analysis will make its parallels with Spanish obvious.

Forms The **conditional tense** is formed with the auxiliary verb *would* plus the infinitive of the main verb.

	SINGULAR	PLURAL
FIRST PERSON	*I would sing*	*we would sing*
SECOND PERSON	*you would sing*	*you would sing*
THIRD PERSON	*he/she would sing*	*they would sing*

The **conditional progressive tense** is formed with the conditional of the verb *to be* plus the present participle. It therefore requires three words.

	SINGULAR	PLURAL
FIRST PERSON	*I would be singing*	*we would be singing*
SECOND PERSON	*you would be singing*	*you would be singing*
THIRD PERSON	*he/she would be singing*	*they would be singing*

Would is often contracted to *'d*.

> *I'd go if you did.*

Uses The conditional is used

1. in Type 2 conditional sentences (*If* CONDITION, *(then)* RESULT.).

   *If I were rich, (then) I **would go** to Europe every year.*

2. to convey the future from a past perspective.

FUTURE	*On Sunday, John said, "OK, I **will** see you on Monday."*
CONDITIONAL	*On Tuesday, Robert says, "John said that he **would** see us on Monday."*

Spanish Conditional tense

Definition In Spanish, the conditional is considered a mood, rather than a tense, since it expresses speculation, not facts. This distinction has, however, no practical effect on its forms or uses.

Forms The conditional tense is formed with the future stem (see page 99). The endings are the same as the imperfect endings for *-er* and *-ir* verbs (see page 95).

hablar (FUTURE hablaré)	perder (FUTURE perderé)	dormir (FUTURE dormiré)
hablaría	perdería	dormiría
hablarías	perderías	dormirías
hablaría	perdería	dormiría
hablaríamos	perderíamos	dormiríamos
hablaríais	perderíais	dormiríais
hablarían	perderían	dormirían

The same verbs that have an irregular stem in the future (see page 99) also have an irregular stem in the conditional, for example, *caber, **cabría**; saber, **sabría**; decir, **diría**.*

Uses Like the English conditional, the conditional in Spanish is used

1. to create Type 2 conditional sentences (*Si* CONDITION [imperfect subjunctive], RESULT [conditional].). (See **Quick Check** on page 111.)

   *Si yo **fuera** rico, **iría** a Europa todos los años.*

2. to convey the future from a past perspective.

*Pablo dice, "Bueno, **estudiaré** mañana."*	Paul says, "OK, I will study tomorrow." (future)
*Andrés dice, "Pablo dijo que **estudiaría** mañana."*	Andrew says, "Paul said he would study tomorrow." (conditional)

3. to make a polite request.

***Querría** ir a Cuba.*	I would like to go to Cuba.

4. to express probability.

***Estarían** muy contentos.*	They were (probably) very happy.

English Perfect tenses

Definition Perfect tenses express

1. the time of the action or state.

2. the fact that it is completed.

"Perfect" in this sense comes from Latin *perfectus,* meaning "finished" or "completed." If something has been perfected, it needs no further work. "Perfect" here, then, does not mean "ideal."

Types There are four perfect tenses corresponding to each of the tenses already discussed: present, past, future, and conditional.

English Present perfect tense

Forms The present perfect tense is formed with the present tense of the verb *to have* plus the past participle of the main verb.

	SINGULAR	PLURAL
FIRST PERSON	*I have sung*	*we have sung*
SECOND PERSON	*you have sung*	*you have sung*
THIRD PERSON	*he/she has sung*	*they have sung*

Uses This tense indicates that from the point of view of the present time, the action has been completed. Compare the following sentences.

> I **saw** that movie yesterday.
> I **have seen** that movie.

The first sentence, using *saw,* stresses a *past* action—what I did yesterday. The second stresses that I am currently experienced with that movie: I now know what it is about, that is, I *have* (present) *seen* (completed, finished with) that movie.

An idiomatic use of this tense is associated with the words *for* and *since.*

> I **have tried for** three hours to phone him.
> I **have tried since** five o'clock to phone him.

In the first sentence, the present perfect tense implies that there is a momentary lull, but the three hours of trying have lasted up to the present.

Perfect (compound) tenses

Forms All perfect tenses in the active voice, except the progressive tenses, are formed with a single auxiliary and the past participle of the main verb. (See page 88 for participle formation.)

Uses In Spanish, there is a perfect tense that corresponds to each of the simple (one-word) tenses.

Present perfect tense

Forms The present perfect is formed with the present tense of the auxiliary verb *haber* plus the past participle of the main verb.

hablar	*perder*	*salir*
he hablado	*he perdido*	*he salido*
has hablado	*has perdido*	*has salido*
ha hablado	*ha perdido*	*ha salido*
hemos hablado	*hemos perdido*	*hemos salido*
habéis hablado	*habéis perdido*	*habéis salido*
han hablado	*han perdido*	*han salido*

WORD ORDER When using the present perfect tense, the conjugated auxiliary verb + past participle of the main verb holds the same position in a Spanish sentence that a simple-tense verb would hold.

✓ **QUICK CHECK**

*Juan lo **dice**.*   *Juan lo **ha dicho**.*
*Juan no lo **dice**.*   *Juan no lo **ha dicho**.*
*¿Se lo **dice**?*   *¿Se lo **ha dicho**?*
*¿No se lo **digo** a Juan?*   *¿No se lo **he dicho** a Juan?*

Uses The present perfect in Spanish is used like it is in English: It refers to an action that took place at an indefinite time in the past or in a time period that began in the past and is still going on. It is used to express an action that still has influence on the present.

***He aprendido** a nadar.*	I have learned to swim. (I do not specify when I learned, and it is something that I can still do.)
*Este año **he aprendido** a nadar.*	This year I have learned to swim. (This year is still going on.)
***He terminado** mis deberes.*	I have finished my homework. (I am still finished with it.)
*Muchos **han leído** las obras de Cervantes.*	Many have read the works of Cervantes. (People have read, and are still reading, Cervantes' works.)
*Hasta ahora, no **he recibido** una carta del presidente.*	Until now, I haven't received a letter from the president. (Up to now I haven't, but I still may.)

CONTINUED ON PAGE 105 ▶

Definition   All progressive tenses emphasize duration, and all are conjugated with the auxiliary verb *to be* plus the present participle of the main verb.

Forms   The present perfect progressive tense in English uses *to be* in the present perfect with the main verb expressed by its present participle.

	SINGULAR	PLURAL
FIRST PERSON	*I have been singing*	*we have been singing*
SECOND PERSON	*you have been singing*	*you have been singing*
THIRD PERSON	*he/she has been singing*	*they have been singing*

Uses   Like other progressive tenses, the present perfect progressive tense emphasizes duration. Consider the following sentences.

> I **have tried** since five o'clock to phone him.
> I **have been trying** for three hours to phone him.

The second sentence stresses how long the three hours have seemed to us.

English   Past perfect (pluperfect) tense

Definition   The past perfect tense indicates that some action (or state) was completed before some other past action (or state).

Forms   The past perfect tense is formed with the simple past tense of the auxiliary verb *to have* plus the past participle of the main verb.

	SINGULAR	PLURAL
FIRST PERSON	*I had sung*	*we had sung*
SECOND PERSON	*you had sung*	*you had sung*
THIRD PERSON	*he/she had sung*	*they had sung*

These forms are often contracted to *I'd, you'd,* and so on.

> I'**d returned** the book before you **asked** for it.

Uses   Think of the past time sequence in terms of "yesterday" (past) and "last week" (further in the past).

> Mary **had finished** her paper before I **began**.
> PAST PERFECT: last week   PAST: yesterday

Spanish Present perfect tense (continued)

Contrast the present perfect tense with the preterite.

> *El año pasado, **aprendí** a nadar.* (Last year is over.)
> ***Terminé** mis tareas.* (The important thing is the past act of finishing, not what is happening now.)
> *Hace dos años, los estudiantes **leyeron** las obras de Cervantes en esa clase.* (We are telling what they did.)
> *No **recibí** nunca una carta del presidente.* (The occasion is past.)

In all of these examples, the emphasis is on actions in the past. For other cases, the imperfect is used. See page 96 for a list contrasting the uses of the preterite and imperfect tenses.

Spanish Present perfect progressive tense

The present perfect progressive tense is formed with the present tense of *haber* plus the past participle of *estar* and the present participle of the main verb.

	SINGULAR	PLURAL
FIRST PERSON	*he estado hablando*	*hemos estado hablando*
SECOND PERSON	*has estado hablando*	*habéis estado hablando*
THIRD PERSON	*ha estado hablando*	*han estado hablando*

Uses As is the case with other progressive tenses, the present perfect progressive emphasizes duration.

***He estado esperándote** más de tres horas.*	I have been waiting for you for more than three hours.
***Uds. han estado quejándose** del trabajo toda la tarde.*	You have been complaining about the work all afternoon.
***Hemos estado pintando** la casa todo el día.*	We have been painting the house all day.

Spanish Past perfect (pluperfect) tense

Forms The past perfect tense in Spanish is formed with the imperfect tense of the auxiliary verb *haber* plus the past participle of the main verb.

AUXILIARY	PAST PARTICIPLE
había	*hablado*
habías	*perdido*
había	*salido*
habíamos	*dicho*
habíais	*visto*
habían	*estado*

Uses Just as in English, the past perfect tense in Spanish refers to an action or state completed in a more remote past than some other past action or state.

English Past perfect progressive tense

Definition   This tense shares characteristics with others that have been introduced. It is

1. past (in terms of time).
2. perfect (in the sense of "completed").
3. progressive (with stress on duration).

Forms   The past perfect progressive tense is formed with the past perfect tense of the verb *to be* plus the present participle of the main verb.

	SINGULAR	PLURAL
FIRST PERSON	*I had been singing*	*we had been singing*
SECOND PERSON	*you had been singing*	*you had been singing*
THIRD PERSON	*he/she had been singing*	*they had been singing*

Uses   This tense expresses an action (or state) that had been continuing just before another past action (or state).

> *I **had been waiting** for three weeks when the letter **arrived**.*

That is, the wait started three weeks ago and continued up to yesterday, when the letter arrived.

spanish Preterite perfect tense

Forms The preterite perfect tense is formed with the preterite of the auxiliary verb *haber* plus the past participle of the verb.

AUXILIARY	PAST PARTICIPLE
hube	*hablado*
hubiste	*perdido*
hubo	*salido*
hubimos	*dicho*
hubisteis	*visto*
hubieron	*estado*

Uses The preterite perfect tense is used primarily in literature. The forms are given here so that you will know them when you come across them in reading. The meanings are the same as for the past perfect, which is more commonly used.

spanish Past perfect progressive tense

Forms The past perfect progressive tense is formed with the imperfect tense of *haber* plus the past participle of *estar* and the present participle of the main verb.

	SINGULAR	PLURAL
FIRST PERSON	*había estado hablando*	*habíamos estado hablando*
SECOND PERSON	*habías estado hablando*	*habíais estado hablando*
THIRD PERSON	*había estado hablando*	*habían estado hablando*

Uses As in English, the past perfect progressive tense expresses an action that had been going on before another past action took place.

> ***Habíamos estado esperando*** *tres meses cuando por fin* **llegó** *la carta.*
>
> We had been waiting for three months when the letter finally arrived.

 # Future perfect tense

Definition This tense expresses an action that will be completed at some time in the future.

Forms The future perfect tense is formed with the future tense of the auxiliary *to have* plus the past participle of the main verb.

	SINGULAR	PLURAL
FIRST PERSON	*I will have sung*	*we will have sung*
SECOND PERSON	*you will have sung*	*you will have sung*
THIRD PERSON	*he/she will have sung*	*they will have sung*

These forms are often contracted, especially in speech, to *I'll've, you'll've,* and so on.

Uses This tense is used to express future completion.

> I **will have finished** the book before the professor **gives** an exam.
> FUTURE PERFECT   PRESENT

In the second clause, the present tense is used in English, even though the verb refers to an action in the future; the professor is not giving an exam now.

Future perfect progressive tense

Definition This tense expresses an action or state that will be continued and then completed in the future.

Forms The future perfect progressive tense is formed with the future perfect tense of the auxiliary *to be* plus the present participle of the main verb.

	SINGULAR	PLURAL
FIRST PERSON	*I will have been singing*	*we will have been singing*
SECOND PERSON	*you will have been singing*	*you will have been singing*
THIRD PERSON	*he/she will have been singing*	*they will have been singing*

Uses This tense is used to emphasize the duration of an action whose beginning point is not specified but whose completion (at least provisionally) will be in the future.

> I **will have been studying** English for 16 years when I **graduate**.
> FUTURE PERFECT PROGRESSIVE   PRESENT

Although graduation is in the future, English uses the present tense. The sentence does not indicate when the speaker will graduate, nor when he or she began to study English. The important point is the relationship between the verbs in the two clauses; 16 years of study will be completed at the moment in the future when I graduate.

spanish Future perfect tense

Forms The future perfect tense is formed with the future tense of the auxiliary verb *haber* plus the past participle.

hablar	*perder*	*salir*
habré hablado	habré perdido	habré salido
habrás hablado	habrás perdido	habrás salido
habrá hablado	habrá perdido	habrá salido
habremos hablado	habremos perdido	habremos salido
habréis hablado	habréis perdido	habréis salido
habrán hablado	habrán perdido	habrán salido

Uses The future perfect tense is used

1. as in English.

2. to express surprise.

   *¿Cómo lo **habrá sabido** Alonso?*   How can Alonso have known?

spanish Future perfect progressive tense

Forms The future perfect progressive tense is formed with the future tense of *haber* plus the past participle of *estar* and the present participle of the main verb.

	SINGULAR	PLURAL
FIRST PERSON	habré estado hablando	habremos estado hablando
SECOND PERSON	habrás estado hablando	habréis estado hablando
THIRD PERSON	habrá estado hablando	habrán estado hablando

Uses The future perfect progressive tense emphasizes the long duration of an action whose beginning is not specified but whose probable completion will be in the future. It is often used to indicate possibility.

__Habrás estado estudiando__ chino toda tu vida, ¿verdad?   You've probably been studying Chinese all your life, right?

¿__Habrá estado trabajando__ Pedro en esa empresa por mucho tiempo?   Is it possible that Peter has been working in that company for a long time?

English Conditional perfect tense

Forms   This tense is formed with the conditional tense of *to have* plus the past participle of the main verb.

	SINGULAR	PLURAL
FIRST PERSON	*I would have sung*	*we would have sung*
SECOND PERSON	*you would have sung*	*you would have sung*
THIRD PERSON	*he/she would have sung*	*they would have sung*

These forms are often contracted, especially in speech, to *I'd've, you'd've,* and so on.

> ***I'd've** come if **I'd** known.*

Uses   This tense is used primarily in the result clauses of Type 3 conditional sentences (see below).

> *He **would have seen** the film if he **had known** that it was so good.*
> *We **would have come** if we   **had known** about it.*
>   CONDITIONAL PERFECT   PAST PERFECT

The *'d* in English can be a contraction of both *had* and *would*. This can cause some confusion unless the meaning of a sentence is analyzed.

> *If he**'d said** he needed it, I**'d have given** it to him.*
>   PLUPEFECT   CONDITIONAL PERFECT

✓ QUICK CHECK

THE THREE MOST COMMON TYPES OF CONDITIONAL SENTENCES IN ENGLISH

if-CLAUSE	RESULT CLAUSE	*if*-CLAUSE	RESULT CLAUSE
1. *If you **are** ready,*	*we **will** go.*	PRESENT	FUTURE
2. *If you **were** ready,*	*we **would** go.*	SUBJUNCTIVE	CONDITIONAL
3. *If you **had been** ready,*	*we **would have** gone.*	PLUPERFECT	CONDITIONAL PERFECT

English Conditional perfect progressive tense

Forms   This tense is formed with the conditional perfect tense of the auxiliary *to be* plus the present participle of the main verb.

	SINGULAR	PLURAL
FIRST PERSON	*I would have been singing*	*we would have been singing*
SECOND PERSON	*you would have been singing*	*you would have been singing*
THIRD PERSON	*he/she would have been singing*	*they would have been singing*

Uses   The conditional perfect progressive tense is used in the same way as the conditional perfect, except that the idea of duration is added.

> *I **would** not **have been sleeping** when you arrived, if I **had known** you were coming.*
>   CONDITIONAL PERFECT PROGRESSIVE   PAST PERFECT

 **Conditional perfect tense**

Forms The conditional perfect tense is formed with the conditional of the auxiliary verb *haber* plus the past participle of the main verb.

hablar	perder	salir
habría hablado	habría perdido	habría salido
habrías hablado	habrías perdido	habrías salido
habría hablado	habría perdido	habría salido
habríamos hablado	habríamos perdido	habríamos salido
habríais hablado	habríais perdido	habríais salido
habrían hablado	habrían perdido	habrían salido

Uses In Spanish, the conditional perfect tense is used, as in English, primarily for Type 3 conditional sentences.

> Él **habría visto** la película, si él **hubiera**   He would have seen the movie if he
>   **sabido** que era tan buena.   had known that it was so good.

✓ QUICK CHECK

THE THREE TYPES OF CONDITIONAL SENTENCES IN SPANISH

if-CLAUSE	RESULT CLAUSE	*if*-CLAUSE	RESULT CLAUSE
1. Si **está** listo,	**iremos** al cine.	PRESENT	FUTURE
2. Si **estuviera** listo,	**iríamos** al cine.	IMPERFECT SUBJUNCTIVE	CONDITIONAL
3. Si **hubiera estado** listo,	**habríamos ido** al cine.	PLUPERFECT SUBJUNCTIVE	CONDITIONAL PERFECT

The imperfect subjunctive forms can have either *-ra* endings (as shown) or *-se* endings. The *-se* forms are used more commonly in Spain than in Latin America.

Spanish Conditional perfect progressive tense

Forms The conditional perfect progressive tense is formed with the conditional of the verb *haber* plus the past participle of *estar* and the present participle of the main verb.

	SINGULAR	PLURAL
FIRST PERSON	habría estado cantando	habríamos estado cantando
SECOND PERSON	habrías estado cantando	habríais estado cantando
THIRD PERSON	habría estado cantando	habrían estado cantando

Uses The conditional perfect progressive tense is used the same way as the conditional perfect, with the additional concept of duration.

> No **habría estado durmiendo** cuando llegaste si **hubiera sabido** que venías.
> CONDITIONAL PERFECT PROGRESSIVE   PLUPERFECT SUBJUNCTIVE

English Passive voice

Definition   The passive voice is used when the subject receives the action of the verb.

ACTIVE VOICE	**The dog**	*bit*	**Susie**.
	SUBJECT	ACTIVE VERB	DIRECT OBJECT
PASSIVE VOICE	**Susie**	was bitten	by **the dog**.
	SUBJECT	PASSIVE VERB	AGENT

Notice that the direct object of the active verb becomes the subject of the passive verb. The active verb's subject is placed after the passive verb in a prepositional phrase and is called the agent. It is not always expressed, as in the colloquial *John got caught*; for such a sentence, it is either not important or not known by whom or what John was caught.

Forms   The passive voice is formed with *to be* or *to get* plus the past participle of the main verb.

Only transitive verbs (ones that have a direct object) can be made passive.

PRESENT	ACTIVE	John **catches** the ball.
	PASSIVE	The ball **is caught** by John.
PAST	ACTIVE	The man **read** the book.
	PASSIVE	The book **was read** by the man.
FUTURE	ACTIVE	Mrs. Smith **will lead** the discussion.
	PASSIVE	The discussion **will be led** by Mrs. Smith.
CONDITIONAL PERFECT	ACTIVE	The class **would have finished** the job, but . . .
	PASSIVE	The job **would have been finished** by the class, but . . .

All the perfect and progressive tenses of the passive voice are formed in the same way. Some forms can be very long and are seldom used; an example of the passive future progressive follows.

*The work **will have been being done** at 3 P.M.*

ꕚꕷꕎꘈꕷꛍ Passive voice

Forms The passive voice in Spanish is formed with the verb *ser* (or sometimes *estar**) plus the past participle of the main verb acting like an adjective, that is, agreeing in gender and number with the subject. The passive voice is used in all tenses, in both indicative and subjunctive moods.

Agency (expressed with English "by") is usually expressed by *por* in Spanish.

PRESENT	ACTIVE	*Juan agarra la pelota.*
	PASSIVE	*La pelota **es agarrada por** Juan.*
PRESENT PERFECT	ACTIVE	*El hombre ha leído los libros.*
	PASSIVE	*Los libros **han sido leídos por** el hombre.*

The agent follows *de* in situations of mental or emotional reactions (less action than response).

*Sus obras **eran reconocidas de** todo*   His works were recognized by
  el mundo.   everyone.

De is also used when neither *ser* nor *estar* is expressed.

*Este maestro, **venerado de** todos los*   This teacher, admired by all the
  estudiantes…   students . . .

In Spanish, the passive voice in all tenses is formed with the appropriate tense of *ser* (or *estar*) plus the past participle of the main verb.

Uses Speakers of Spanish prefer the active voice to the passive. Sometimes authors use less vivid language when writing in the passive. Compare the following English sentences.

| PASSIVE | Our receiver was tackled by their defensive end. |
| ACTIVE | Their defensive end slammed our receiver to the ground. |

| PASSIVE | This abstract was painted by Pablo Picasso. |
| ACTIVE | Pablo Picasso created this colorful abstract. |

When the agent is not known, or when the result is more important than the action, the passive voice is sufficient.

*La casa **está destruida**.*   The house is destroyed.
*El poema **fue escrito** por Bécquer.*   The poem was written by Bécquer.

Most of the time, however, it is better to use the active voice. There are a number of ways to avoid the passive voice in Spanish.

1. Turn the sentence around.

    NOT *El libro **fue leído por** la clase.*
    BUT *La clase **leyó** el libro.*

2. Use an impersonal construction.

    NOT *Aquí el español **es hablado**.*
    BUT ***Se habla** español.*

3. Use the reflexive.

    NOT *Ayer los vestidos **eran vendidos** a bajo precio.*
    BUT ***Ayer** los vestidos **se vendían** a bajo precio.*

---

* *Estar* is used to form the passive when neither the agent nor the action is of any real importance. The past participle is, in effect, an adjective describing a condition or the result of a past action

*El apartamento **estaba** muy mal **amueblado**.*   The apartment was very badly furnished.

English Imperative mood

Definition   The imperative mood is the mood used to give commands.

Forms   The forms of the English imperative are very similar to those of the present indicative, with a few exceptions.

The second-person imperative (both singular and plural) has only one form: *Sing!*

For the first-person plural, the auxiliary verb *let* is used.

> *Let's sing!*

For the third-person (singular and plural), the auxiliary verbs *let, have,* and *make* are used.

> *Let her sing!*
> *Have them come in!*
> *Make him stop!*

No subject is expressed in an imperative sentence.

IRREGULAR IMPERATIVES English has only one irregular imperative: for the verb *to be*. Compare the following sentences.

INDICATIVE	IMPERATIVE
You are good.	*Be good!*
We are quiet.	*Let's be quiet!*

Forms   In the Spanish imperative, there are special forms for the affirmative *tú* and *vosotros* commands: The *tú* form drops the *-s* of the indicative; the *vosotros* form is identical to the infinitive, except that *-d* replaces *-r*.

All other imperative forms, including the third-person affirmative commands and the negative *tú* and *vosotros* commands, use the present subjunctive (see page 117).

AFFIRMATIVE COMMANDS

	hablar	*comer*	*vivir*
TÚ	*¡habla!*	*¡come!*	*¡vive!*
VOSOTROS, VOSOTRAS	*¡hablad!*	*¡comed!*	*¡vivid!*
NOSOTROS, NOSOTRAS	*¡hablemos!*	*¡comamos!*	*¡vivamos!*
USTED	*¡hable!*	*¡coma!*	*¡viva!*
USTEDES	*¡hablen!*	*¡coman!*	*¡vivan!*

NEGATIVE COMMANDS

	hablar	*comer*	*vivir*
TÚ	*¡no hables!*	*¡no comas!*	*¡no vivas!*
VOSOTROS, VOSOTRAS	*¡no habléis!*	*¡no comáis!*	*¡no viváis!*

As would be expected, negative commands have the word *no* placed before the affirmative command for the *nosotros/nosotras*, *usted*, and *ustedes* forms.

IRREGULAR IMPERATIVES   Some verbs have irregular forms in the imperative mood.

	decir	*hacer*	*ir*
TÚ	*di*	*haz*	*ve*
USTED	*diga*	*haga*	*vaya*
NOSOTROS, NOSOTRAS	*digamos*	*hagamos*	*vayamos*
VOSOTROS, VOSOTRAS	*decid*	*haced*	*id*
USTEDES	*digan*	*hagan*	*vayan*

WORD ORDER   In affirmative commands, pronoun subjects (if expressed) follow the verb.

¡Hablen (ustedes) *español!*	Speak Spanish!
¡Ven (tú) *conmigo!*	Come with me!

Pronoun object(s), if any, are attached to the verb (see pages 23 and 25).

*¡Díga***me***!*	Tell me!
*¡Escríba***lo***!*	Write it!
*¡Vámo***nos***!*	Let's go!

In negative commands, the objects appear in normal position and order.

¡No **me** *diga!*	Don't tell me!
¡No **lo** *escriba!*	Don't write it!
¡No **nos** *vayamos!*	Let's not go!

Subjunctive mood

Definition   The subjunctive is the mood that expresses what may be true.

Forms   The **present subjunctive** (or the auxiliary verb in a compound tense) has the same form for all persons: the basic (infinitive) form of the verb. It is different from the indicative only for

1. the third-person singular.

   that he take
   that she have

2. the verb *to be*.

   PRESENT   *that I be, that he be*
   PAST   *that I were, that she were*

CONTINUED ON PAGE 118 ▶

Forms In Spanish, there are four commonly used tenses in the subjunctive mood: the present subjunctive, the imperfect subjunctive, the present perfect subjunctive, and the past perfect (pluperfect) subjunctive. The present subjunctive is formed as follows.

STEM Drop the -o of the first-person singular.

ENDINGS Add the appropriate endings for either -ar verbs or -er/-ir verbs from the chart that follows.

The dominant vowel of -ar verbs becomes e, and the dominant vowel of both -er and -ir verbs becomes a.

hablar (yo hablo)	comer (yo como)	abrir (yo abro)
hable	coma	abra
hables	comas	abras
hable	coma	abra
hablemos	comamos	abramos
habléis	comáis	abráis
hablen	coman	abran

Because the stem of the present subjunctive is taken from the *yo* form of the present indicative, the present subjunctive stem reflects any changes in those first-person forms.

1. Stem-changing verbs: *pensar, **pie**nse; volver, **vue**lva; pedir, **pi**da.*

2. Spanish verbs whose *yo* form ends in -go: *distinguir, distin**ga**; poner, pon**ga**.* Other verbs that show the same change are *seguir, salir, hacer, decir, tener, oír.*

3. Stem-changing verbs like *seguir* that drop the *u* of the infinitive to reflect the hard *g* sound: *seguir, **si**ga.*

4. Verbs with an irregular *yo* form in the present indicative: *conocer, cono**zca**; escoger, esco**ja**.*

Spelling changes in subjunctive forms are seen in verbs ending in -car and -gar. In verbs ending in -car, *c* changes to *qu* before an *e*, and in verbs ending in -gar, *g* changes to *gu* before *e*: *tocar, to**que**; pagar, pa**gue**.*

IRREGULAR PRESENT SUBJUNCTIVES Some common verbs are irregular in the present subjunctive.

INFINITIVE	IRREGULAR STEM PLUS ENDINGS
haber	haya, hayas, haya; hayamos, hayáis, hayan
ser	sea, seas, sea; seamos, seáis, sean
ir	vaya, vayas, vaya; vayamos, vayáis, vayan
estar	esté, estés, esté; estemos, estéis, estén
dar	dé, des, dé; demos, deis, den
saber	sepa, sepas, sepa; sepamos, sepáis, sepan
ver	vea, veas, vea; veamos, veáis, vean

CONTINUED ON PAGE 119 ▶

Uses The subjunctive is rarely used in English. For that reason, it tends to be disregarded except in certain fixed expressions. Nevertheless, it does have some specific uses that are important in formal English.

1. In contrary-to-fact conditions

   *If I **were** you . . .*
   *"If this **be** madness, yet there is method in it." (Hamlet)*

2. After verbs like *wish, suppose, insist, urge, demand, ask, recommend,* and *suggest*

   *I wish that he **were** able to come.*
   *They insisted that we **be** present.*
   *I recommend that she **learn** the subjunctive.*

3. After some impersonal expressions, such as *it is necessary* and *it is important*

   *It is important that he **avoid** errors.*
   *It is necessary that Mary **see** its importance.*

4. In certain fixed expressions

   *So **be** it!*
   *Long **live** the Queen!*
   *Heaven **forbid**!*
   *Far **be** it from me to suggest that!*

Most of these fixed expressions express a third-person imperative; the idea "I wish that" is implied, but not expressed.

Except for the fixed expressions, English speakers tend to use an alternative expression whenever possible, usually with modal verbs (auxiliaries), to avoid the subjunctive in conversation and informal writing. Compare the following sentences with the examples above.

*I wish that he **could come**.*
*I told her that she **must learn** the subjunctive.*
*It is important for him **to avoid** errors.*
*Mary **needs to see** its importance.*

Uses   In theory, the subjunctive is used to show that what is being said is

1. potentially (but not actually) true.

2. colored by emotion (which often distorts facts).

3. expressing an attitude toward something (rather than the actual facts).

4. doubtful, probably nonexistent, or not true.

In practice, there are certain words and expressions that require the subjunctive. The theory may help you remember which words and expressions they are, but you cannot argue theory against practice. If an expression requires the subjunctive, then it must be used whether or not you believe it fits well into the theoretical bases.

The subjunctive is used principally

1. after verbs or other expressions conveying the subject's emotional reactions.

> *Estoy contento que...*
> *Tememos que...*
> *Me sorprende que...*

2. after verbs such as *querer* and *exigir* when there is a change of subject.

SUBJUNCTIVE   *Quiero que Raúl venga.* (change of subject)
INFINITIVE   *Quiero venir.* (no change of subject)

3. after verbs of doubt, negation, necessity, importance, and opinion when uncertainty is conveyed. Compare the following lists.

SUBJUNCTIVE	INDICATIVE
Dudo que mi padre *venga*.	*Estoy cierto* que mi madre *viene*.
Niega que este hombre *sea* su padre.	*Es verdad* que este hombre *es* su padre.
Es posible que yo no *venga*.	*Es cierto* que yo no *vengo*.
Es increíble que él no me *crea*.	*Es seguro* que él me *cree*.
Ojalá que *venga*.	*Es cierto* que *viene*.
Es bueno que tú no *tengas* hambre.	Tú no *tienes* hambre.
Es importante que ustedes *aprendan* el español.	Ustedes *aprenden* el español.

4. after conjunctions expressing

   a. concession: *aunque, bien que.*

   b. purpose: *porque, a fin de que.*

   c. indefinite time: *hasta que, antes de que.*

   d. negation: *sin que, a menos que.*

5. after superlatives (because of possible emotional exaggeration). Compare the following statements.

> *Es el mejor poema que* **conozca**.   It's the best poem I know.
>   (I really like it!)
>
> *Es el joven más alto que yo* **conozco**.   He's the tallest young man I know.
>   (None of my other friends are so tall.)

The first statement conveys an emotion; the second states a fact. The indicative and subjunctive respectively tell the audience how the statement is meant. Some Spanish speakers do not make this distinction and use the subjunctive in all cases.

CONTINUED ON PAGE 120 ▶

Spanish Subjunctive mood (continued)

6. after relative pronouns referring to an indefinite antecedent.

*Quiero hablar con **alguien que conozca** bien la ciudad.*	I want to talk with someone who knows the city well.

7. after verbs (such as *pensar* and *creer*) that take the subjunctive in the negative or interrogative. To ask what someone thinks or to say what someone does not believe implies doubt about the true situation. The negative interrogative requires the indicative, however, when a positive response is expected.

*¿Cree Ud. que el profesor **esté** enfermo?*	Do you believe that the professor is ill? (implied doubt)
*No creo que el profesor **esté** enfermo.*	I don't believe that the professor is ill. (implied doubt)
*¿No cree Ud. que el profesor **esté** enfermo?*	Don't you believe that the professor is ill? (implied doubt)
*¿No cree Ud. que el profesor **está** enfermo?*	Don't you believe that the professor is ill? (positive response expected)

8. for third-person commands.

*¡Que **se callen**!*	Let them be quiet!

Compare this third-person command with the imperative mood, page 115.

9. in certain fixed expressions.

*¡**Viva** el Rey!*	Long live the King!

To remember the principal uses of the subjunctive, think of the mnemonic "**NEEDS PAWS.**"

Necessity
Emotion
Exaggeration
Demanding
Seeming

Possibility
Asking
Wishing
Supposing

Forms The imperfect subjunctive is formed as follows.

STEM Drop the *-ron* ending of the third-person plural preterite.

ENDINGS Add appropriate endings from the chart that follows; form I endings are more commonly used. Note that the *nosotros* form endings take a written accent.

FORM I

estudiar	comer	abrir	decir
estudiara	comiera	abriera	dijera
estudiaras	comieras	abrieras	dijeras
estudiara	comiera	abriera	dijera
estudiáramos	comiéramos	abriéramos	dijéramos
estudiarais	comierais	abrierais	dijerais
estudiaran	comieran	abrieran	dijeran

FORM II

estudiar	comer	abrir	decir
estudiase	comiese	abriese	dijese
estudiases	comieses	abrieses	dijeses
estudiase	comiese	abriese	dijese
estudiásemos	comiésemos	abriésemos	dijésemos
estudiaseis	comieseis	abrieseis	dijeseis
estudiasen	comiesen	abriesen	dijesen

Form II endings are generally limited to formal writing, though they are used in everyday speech in Spain. Form II endings are included here so that you will be able to recognize them.

A future subjunctive exists in Spanish, though it is rarely used and is not being introduced here.

There is no conditional subjunctive in Spanish. The imperfect subjunctive is used when a conditional idea is expressed. *CIF*

Uses The imperfect subjunctive appears in a subordinate clause when

1. a verb in the main clause that requires a subjunctive is in the past.

Los estudiantes **temían** *que el profesor* **estuviera** *enfermo.*	The students were afraid that the professor was sick.

2. a verb in the main clause that requires a subjunctive is in the present indicative, but the idea expressed by the subordinate clause is in the past tense.

Es bueno *que él* **llegara** *ayer.*	It's good that he arrived yesterday.

has / have modal/aux.

Forms The present perfect subjunctive is formed with the present subjunctive of the auxiliary verb *haber* plus the past participle of the main verb.

AUXILIARY	PAST PARTICIPLE
haya	*hablado*
hayas	*perdido*
haya	*salido*
hayamos	*dicho*
hayáis	*visto*
hayan	*estado*

Uses When a verb is governed by a verbal or other expression that requires the subjunctive, the present perfect subjunctive is used in a subordinate clause that expresses action that has taken place or that may have taken place.

Espero que el profesor *haya leído* nuestros exámenes.	I hope the professor has read our exams.
Aunque el profesor *haya leído* los exámenes, eso no quiere decir que hoy él va a devolvérselos a los estudiantes.	Although the professor may have read the exams, that doesn't mean that he's going to return them to the students today.
Cuando usted *haya decidido*, dígamelo por favor.	When you have decided, please tell me.

has / have modal / aux.

Past perfect (pluperfect) subjunctive *had/would have* *modal/aux.*

Forms   The past perfect (pluperfect) subjunctive is formed with the imperfect subjunctive of the auxiliary verb *haber* and the past participle of the verb.

FORM I

AUXILIARY	PAST PARTICIPLE
hubiera	estudiado
hubieras	comido
hubiera	vivido
hubiéramos	abierto
hubierais	dicho
hubieran	visto

FORM II

AUXILIARY	PAST PARTICIPLE
hubiese	estudiado
hubieses	comido
hubiese	vivido
hubiésemos	salido
hubieseis	dicho
hubiesen	visto

Uses   When a verb is governed by a verbal or other expression that requires the subjunctive, the past perfect subjunctive is used in subordinate clauses that express an action that has occurred prior to the action of the verb in the main clause.

Temían que Alicia **hubiera partido**.   They were afraid that Alice had left.

No **creí** que Ramón **hubiera mentido**.   I did not believe that Raymond had lied. ("would have lied")

Yo no **habría creído** *que el profesor* **hubiera podido hacer** *lo que había hecho.*   I would not have believed that the professor could have done what he had done.

had/would have: modal/aux.

Exercises

The following exercises, grouped by part of speech, test your grasp of key grammatical aspects of Spanish. As a reminder of the similarities and differences between Spanish and English, a cross-reference is provided at the end of each exercise to the relevant grammar points discussed in this book. An answer key is provided after the appendices.

Nouns

A *Add the correct definite article before each of the following Spanish nouns.*

1. _____ clase
2. _____ libro
3. _____ azúcar
4. _____ agua
5. _____ aguas

6. _____ padres
7. _____ coches
8. _____ guerra
9. _____ lápiz
10. _____ mesa

◀ *For more help, see* Introducing determiners, *page 17.*

B *Add the correct indefinite article before each of the following Spanish nouns.*

1. _____ casa
2. _____ pared
3. _____ ventanas
4. _____ suelo
5. _____ techo

6. _____ habitaciones
7. _____ escalera
8. _____ sótano
9. _____ cocina
10. _____ muebles

◀ *For more help, see* Introducing determiners, *pages 17–18.*

C *Complete each of the following sentences with the correct definite or indefinite article.*

1. ¿Hay _____ restaurantes por aquí?

2. Sí, _____ restaurantes de este barrio son muy buenos.

3. ¿_____ comida es cara en esos restaurantes?

4. _____ restaurantes son caros, otros no.

5. ¿Hay _____ restaurante mexicano en el barrio?

6. Oh, sí. _____ restaurante mexicano es uno de mis restaurantes favoritos.

7. _____ platos que sirven son auténticos y muy variados.

8. Me gustaría comer _____ enchiladas.

9. En ese caso, vamos allí ahora. _____ enchiladas que sirven son las mejores que he probado.

10. Y yo voy a pedir _____ tacos también.

◀ *For more help, see* Introducing determiners, *pages 17–18.*

Pronouns

A *What subject pronoun can go with each of these present tense verb forms? List all possibilities.*

1. hablamos _____

2. escribo _____

3. vende _____

4. estáis _____

5. bailan _____

6. es _____

7. puedo _____

8. eres _____

9. vivís _____

10. ponen _____

11. comes _____

12. hacemos _____

◀ *For more help, see* Personal pronouns, *page 23.*

B *Rewrite each of the following sentences, replacing the italicized direct object noun with the corresponding direct object pronoun.*

1. Tenemos *los disquetes.* _____

2. Preparan *la cena.* _____

3. Reparo *las computadoras.* _____

4. ¿No bebes *el jugo*? _____

5. No conocen *a María Elena.* _____

6. Ya leí *las revistas.* _____

7. Llevamos *a los niños* al zoológico. _____

8. ¿Compraron Uds. *los regalos*? _____

9. Vendieron *su coche.* _____

10. El niño rompió *el juguete.* _____

◀ *For more help, see* Personal pronouns, *pages 23 and 25.*

C *Rewrite each of the following sentences, replacing the italicized direct object noun with the corresponding direct object pronoun. Each sentence with an infinitive has two possibilities.*

1. Haz *el café.* _____

2. No sirvas *los pasteles.* _____

3. Quiero comer *la torta.* _____

_____

4. ¿Debo cerrar *la puerta?* _____

_____

5. Pongan *los libros* en la mesa. _____

6. Abra *las ventanas.* _____

7. ¿Podemos ver *las fotos?* _____

_____

8. Los estudiantes piensan estudiar *el texto.* _____

_____

9. ¿Puede Ud. traducir *este mensaje?* _____

_____

10. Saca *la basura.* _____   _____

◀ *For more help, see* Personal pronouns, *pages 23 and 25.*

D *Complete each of the following exchanges with the correct direct object pronoun.*

1. SR. GÓMEZ ¿Ud. me conoce, señora?

   SRA. GÓMEZ No, señor. No _____ conozco.

2. AMALIA ¿Pablo te va a invitar?

   CARLA No sé si va a invitar _____.

3. ABUELA ¿El tío Francisco les escribe?

   NIÑOS Sí, _____ escribe todas las semanas.

4. CARLOS ¿Te molesto?

   LILIANA No, no _____ molestas.

5. FEDERICO ¿Sabes si Lucas desea hablar conmigo?

   ANA Sí, creo que _____ busca.

◀ *For more help, see* Personal pronouns, *pages 23 and 25.*

E *Rewrite the following sentences, replacing the italicized words with the correct direct and indirect object pronouns. Each sentence will have two object pronouns.*

1. Les envían *los regalos a sus padres.* _____

2. Le lee *el cuento a su hija.* _____

3. Dales *los juguetes a los niños.* _____

4. Les mando *el dinero a mis primos.* _____

5. ¿Puedes devolverme *los cien dólares?* _____

6. Les enseña *el español a los estudiantes.* _____

7. Te voy a mostrar *las fotos.* _____

8. A Ud. le voy a vender *mi coche.* _____

9. Me pongo *el abrigo.* _____

10. Dígame *la verdad.* _____

11. Voy a prepararte *el café.* _____

12. ¿Les explicas *la lección a tus amigos?* _____

◀ *For more help, see* Personal pronouns, *pages 23, 25, and 27.*

F *Complete each of the following sentences with the correct disjunctive pronoun.*

1. A _____ no nos gusta este barrio.

2. ¿Y a _____ qué te gusta comer?

3. A _____ me gustan mucho los tacos.

4. Este regalo es para _____, señora. Espero que le guste.

5. Uds. no lo invitaron a la fiesta. Por eso él está enojado con _____.

6. Tú nunca piensas en _____. Nunca me llamas, nunca me vienes a ver.

◀ *For more help, see* Personal pronouns, *page 25;* Disjunctive pronouns, *page 33.*

G *Complete the following Spanish sentences so that they match the English sentences in meaning.*

1. I like my bicycle, but he prefers his.

   A mí me gusta la bicicleta mía, pero él prefiere _____.

2. This house is older than ours.

   Esta casa es más antigua que _____.

3. These books aren't María's, they're mine.

   Estos libros no son los de María, son _____.

4. I have my notes. Do you have yours?

   Yo tengo mis notas. ¿Tienes _____?

5. She needs my pencil because she has lost hers.

   Ella necesita el lápiz mío porque ha perdido _____.

6. My car is broken down. Can you take yours?

   Tengo el coche descompuesto. ¿Puede Ud. llevar _____?

7. I brought my photos, and they brought theirs.

   Yo traje las fotos mías y ellos trajeron _____.

8. Our dog is bigger than theirs.

   Nuestro perro es más grande que _____.

9. I like your class. It's better than mine.

   Me gusta tu clase. Es mejor que _____.

10. I forgot my diskettes. Could you lend me yours?

    Se me olvidaron mis disquetes. ¿Podría Ud. prestarme _____?

11. I think my report is longer than yours.

    Creo que el informe mío es más largo que _____.

12. First we'll go to his house and then to mine.

    Primero iremos a la casa de él y después a _____.

◀ *For more help, see* Possessive pronouns, *page 29.*

H   *Select the correct relative pronoun to complete each of the following sentences.*

1. Aquí tienes el artículo _____ he leído.
   a. que   b. quien   c. quienes   d. lo que   e. cuyo

2. Voy a presentarte al colega con _____ yo trabajaba antes.
   a. que   b. quien   c. quienes   d. lo que   e. cuyo

3. Éstos son los niños para _____ he comprado los juguetes.
   a. que   b. quien   c. quienes   d. lo que   e. cuyo

4. No comprendemos _____ quieres.
   a. que   b. quien   c. quienes   d. lo que   e. cuyo

5. Ésta es la señora _____ trabaja aquí.
   a. que   b. quien   c. quienes   d. lo que   e. cuyo

6. Eso es _____ me sorprendió.
   a. que   b. quien   c. quienes   d. lo que   e. cuyo

7. El escritor _____ libro leí es muy famoso.
   a. que   b. quien   c. quienes   d. lo que   e. cuyo

8. El ingeniero de _____ Ud. habló es muy inteligente.
   a. que   b. quien   c. quienes   d. lo que   e. cuyo

◀ *For more help, see* Relative pronouns, *page 35.*

I *Translate the following phrases and sentences into Spanish, using demonstrative pronouns.*

1. This book and that one (near you).

   _____

2. These houses and those (over there).

   _____

3. These restaurants are good, but those (over there) are better.

   _____

4. That cell phone (near you) (*teléfono celular*) is good, but this one is excellent.

   _____

5. I like cars, but I don't like that one (over there).

   _____

6. These gardens and those (near you) have beautiful flowers.

   _____

7. Do you (*tú*) want those pastries (over there) or these?

   _____

8. That bicycle (near you) is more expensive than this one.

   _____

◀ *For more help, see* Demonstrative pronouns, *page 39.*

J *Complete the following Spanish sentences so that they match the English sentences in meaning.*

1. Whom are you writing to?

   ¿_____ le escribes?

2. What are you looking for?

   ¿_____ buscan Uds.?

3. Whom [which people] did you invite?

   ¿_____ invitaste?

4. I like these two cars. Which is less expensive?

   Me gustan estos dos coches. ¿_____ es menos caro?

5. What is the child afraid of?

   ¿_____ tiene miedo el niño?

6. Whom is she going out with?

   ¿_____ sale ella?

7. What are you thinking about?

   ¿_____ piensas tú?

8. There are so many newspapers. How many do you read?

   Hay tantos periódicos. ¿_____ _____ lee Ud.?

9. Who works there?

   ¿_____ trabaja allí?

10. What have you done?

    ¿_____ has hecho?

11. Whom did you see?

    ¿_____ has visto?

12. How much sugar do you need?

    ¿_____ azúcar necesitas?

13. Whom [which people] are these gifts for?

    ¿_____ son estos regalos?

14. Here are several computers. Which ones do you prefer?

    Aquí hay varias computadoras. ¿_____ prefieres?

◀ For more help, see Interrogative pronouns, pages 41–42.

Adjectives

A   *Complete each of the following lists with the missing form of the adjective.*

1. a. un libro _____

   b. una historia _____ _____

   c. libros <u>interesantes</u>

   d. historias _____

2. a. un árbol <u>blanco</u>

   b. una flor _____

   c. árboles _____

   d. flores _____

3. a. un hombre _____

   b. una mujer _____ _____

   c. unos hombres <u>españoles</u>

   d. unas mujeres _____

4. a. un pueblo <u>andaluz</u>

   b. una ciudad _____

   c. pueblos _____

   d. ciudades _____

5. a. un _____ libro

 b. una _____ revista

 c. ___buenos___ libros

 d. _____ revistas

6. a. un muchacho _____

 b. una muchacha ___joven___

 c. unos muchachos _____

 d. unas muchachas _____

7. a. un examen ___fácil___

 b. una tarea _____

 c. unos exámenes _____

 d. unas tareas _____

8. a. _____ monumento

 b. _____ estatua

 c. ___algunos___ monumentos

 d. _____ estatuas

9. a. un restaurant _____

 b. una cerveza _____

 c. restaurantes _____

 d. cervezas ___alemanas___

10. a. un _____ profesor

 b. una _____ profesora

 c. _____ profesores

 d. ___grandes___ profesoras

◀ *For more help, see* Descriptive adjectives, *pages 46–47.*

B *Complete each of the following phrases according to the English cue in parentheses.*

1. (*third*) el _____ día

2. (*no*) _____ posibilidad

3. (*bad*) un _____ momento

4. (*first*) mi _____ idea

5. (*some*) _____ acontecimiento

6. (*great*) un _____ científico

7. (*third*) la _____ parada

8. (*no*) _____ curso

9. (*first*) su _____ viaje

10. (*good*) un _____ amigo

◄ *For more help, see* Descriptive adjectives, *pages 46–47;* Limiting adjectives, *page 50.*

C *Complete each of the following phrases with the correct form of* Santo.

1. _____ José   6. _____ María

2. _____ Ana   7. _____ Domingo

3. _____ Tomás   8. _____ Lucas

4. _____ Lucía   9. _____ Bárbara

5. _____ Pedro   10. _____ Antonio

◄ *For more help, see* Descriptive adjectives, *page 47.*

D *Translate the following phrases into Spanish.*

1. a poor (unfortunate) man _____

2. a friend [fem.] of many years _____

3. a former general _____

4. an ancient city _____

5. a great woman _____

6. a poor (penniless) man _____

7. a tall girl _____

8. an elderly neighbor [masc.] _____

◄ *For more help, see* Descriptive adjectives, *page 47.*

E *Translate the following sentences into Spanish.*

1. Jaime is more intelligent than Raúl.

_____

2. My sister is less studious (*aplicada*) than my brother.

_____

3. It's the best book in the library.

_____

4. The subway is faster than the bus.

_____

5. He is the worst student at the school.

_____

6. My course is less interesting than their course.

_____

◀ _For more help, see_ Comparison of adjectives, _pages 48–49._

F   _Translate the following phrases into Spanish. Each phrase contains a demonstrative adjective._

1. those women (over there)   _____

2. this book   _____

3. that table   _____

4. those planes   _____

5. that car (over there)   _____

6. these chairs   _____

7. those windows   _____

8. that door (over there)   _____

9. this page   _____

10. those buses (over there)   _____

11. those trains   _____

12. these exams   _____

◀ _For more help, see_ Demonstrative adjectives, _page 51._

G   _Translate the following phrases into Spanish._

1. her book   _____

2. my school   _____

3. his house   _____

4. our translation   _____

5. their gardens   _____

6. your (_tú_) ideas   _____

7. your (_Uds._) notebooks   _____

8. my homework assignments   _____

9. your (_tú_) composition   _____

10. his story   _____

◀ _For more help, see_ Possessive adjectives, _page 53._

Adverbs

A *Write the adverb that corresponds to each of the following adjectives.*

1. fácil _____

2. nervioso _____

3. maravilloso _____

4. bueno _____

5. lento _____

6. claro _____

7. natural _____

8. cuidadoso _____

9. responsable _____

10. feroz _____

◀ *For more help, see* Introducing adverbs, *page 61.*

B *Translate the following negative sentences into Spanish.*

1. He doesn't work. _____

2. He doesn't work anymore. _____

3. He never works. _____

4. No one works. _____

5. She is not learning anything. _____

6. We don't see Paula or Carmen. _____

◀ *For more help, see* Introducing adverbs, *page 63.*

Prepositions

A *Complete each of the following sentences with the Spanish equivalent of the preposition in parentheses.*

1. (*to*) Ella va _____ España.

2. (*near*) Vivimos _____ la plaza.

3. (*in*) Trabajan _____ México.

4. (*in front of*) Hay un jardín _____ mi casa.

5. (*under*) Están sentados _____ un árbol.

6. (*before*) Vinieron _____ las tres.

◀ *For more help, see* Introducing prepositions, *page 75.*

B *Add the correct preposition before the infinitive in each of the following sentences. If no preposition is required, write an X.*

1. Él está aquí. Acabo _____ verlo.

2. Voy _____ buscarlo, entonces.

3. Mi habitación da _____ la calle.

4. No sé si puedo _____ ir.

5. Llegaron _____ respetarlo.

6. Lo vi cuando miré _____ la ventana.

7. No te pongas _____ llorar.

8. Trato _____ comprenderlo.

9. Vino _____ decirme que no podía ir.

10. ¿Qué quieres _____ hacer?

11. ¿Por qué se ríen Uds. _____ mí?

12. Hoy empecé _____ estudiar para el examen.

◀ *For more help, see* Introducing prepositions, *page 77.*

Verbs

A *Complete the following chart with the present and past participles of each infinitive.*

INFINITIVE	PRESENT PARTICIPLE	PAST PARTICIPLE
1. decir	_____	_____
2. ir	_____	_____
3. ver	_____	_____
4. morir	_____	_____
5. abrir	_____	_____
6. poner	_____	_____
7. sentir	_____	_____
8. dormir	_____	_____
9. escribir	_____	_____
10. romper	_____	_____
11. hacer	_____	_____
12. volver	_____	_____

◀ *For more help, see* Participles, *pages 87–88.*

B *Complete each of the following sentences with the present tense form of the verb in parentheses.*

1. (caminar)   Los muchachos _____ rápidamente.

2. (aprender) Yo _____ mucho en esta clase.

3. (entender) ¿_____ (tú) lo que te dicen?

4. (pensar)   Ellos _____ irse de vacaciones.

5. (sentir)   ¿Te molesté? ¡Cuánto lo _____!

6. (mostrar)   ¿Por qué no me _____ (tú) tus fotos?

7. (jugar)   Los niños _____ en el parque.

8. (pedir)   Él siempre me _____ ayuda.

9. (repetir)   Ella siempre _____ la misma cosa.

10. (permitir) Nosotros no te lo _____.

11. (comer)   Hoy (nosotros) _____ en el centro.

12. (seguir)   Yo _____ en la misma clase.

13. (hacer)   ¿Qué _____ yo ahora?

14. (traer)   Espera y yo te lo _____.

15. (estar)   Yo no _____ enojado.

◀ *For more help, see* Present tense, *pages 91–93.*

C *Write the present progressive form that is equivalent to each of the following present tense forms.*

1. trabaja   _____

2. vuelvo   _____

3. escribes   _____

4. camina   _____

5. pedimos   _____

6. duermen   _____

7. oigo   _____

8. mientes   _____

◀ *For more help, see* Present tense, *pages 91–93.*

D *Rewrite the following sentences, using the imperfect tense.* (indicativo)

1. Habla con su novia.   _____

2. Terminamos nuestro trabajo. _____

3. Ella hace un café.   _____

4. Espero a mis amigos.   _____

5. El niño duerme.   _____

6. Estamos preocupados. _____

7. Vendes tu casa. _____

8. Ella trabaja en esta oficina. _____

9. Estudiamos nuestras lecciones. _____

10. Siguen por esta calle. _____

11. Van al centro. _____

12. Veo películas en la tele. _____

13. Escribes una carta. _____

14. Ud. lee mucho. _____

15. Salgo. _____

16. Ella está en el centro. _____

17. Es inteligente. _____

18. Nunca pierdes nada. _____

◀ For more help, see Imperfect tense, page 95.

E Write the imperfect progressive that is equivalent to each of the following imperfect tense forms.

1. comían _____

2. veías _____

3. éramos _____

4. yo hablaba _____

5. salíamos _____

6. regresaban _____

7. ella llegaba _____

8. vivías _____

◀ For more help, see Imperfect tense, page 95.

F Complete each of the following sentences with the correct preterite form of the verb in parentheses.

1. (comprar) Nosotros no _____ nada en el centro.

2. (prender) ¿(Tú) _____ la tele?

3. (buscar) Lo _____ pero no lo encontré.

4. (tener) Yo _____ que salir.

5. (sentirse) Ella _____ mal.

6. (dormir) ¿Ud. no _____ bien?

7. (escribir)   ¿(Tú) _____ la carta?

8. (empezar)   Yo _____ a estudiar anoche.

9. (poner)   ¿Qué _____ Juan en la mochila?

10. (hacer)   ¿Qué _____ Sonia ayer?

11. (decir)   Ellos no me _____ nada.

12. (traducir)   ¿Quién _____ el mensaje?

13. (venir)   ¿A qué hora _____ tus amigos?

14. (ser)   El verano _____ bueno.

15. (saber)   ¿Cuándo _____ tú que él no iba a venir?

16. (querer)   Me invitaron, pero no _____ ir.

17. (dar)   Yo no me _____ cuenta de nada.

18. (pagar)   Yo _____ la cuenta.

19. (comer)   Nosotros _____ en casa ayer.

20. (dar)   ¿Qué regalos te _____ tus abuelos?

21. (estar)   ¡Qué rico _____ la comida!

22. (caminar)   Ellos _____ una hora.

23. (ir)   ¿(Tú) _____ en avión?

24. (poder)   Queríamos ir, pero no _____ .

◀ *For more help, see* Preterite tense, *page 97.*

G   *Answer each of the following questions with* No sé si + *future tense, as in the model.*

MODELO   ¿Juan va a terminar?   *No sé si terminará.*

1. ¿Ellos van a salir?   _____

2. ¿Voy a poder?   _____

3. ¿Nuestro equipo va a perder?   _____

4. ¿Vas a hacerlo?   _____

5. ¿Uds. van a saberlo?   _____

6. ¿Lo vas a decir?   _____

7. ¿Ud. va a abrir la puerta?   _____

8. ¿Uds. van a poner la mesa?   _____

9. ¿Va a haber una reunión?   _____

10. ¿Voy a querer?   _____

◀ *For more help, see* Future tense, *page 99.*

H Complete each of the following sentences with the correct conditional form of the verb in parentheses.

1. (tener) Yo creía que los niños _____ hambre.

2. (poner) Si pudiera escoger, me _____ la otra corbata.

3. (echar) Ella sabía que nosotros _____ la carta al correo.

4. (hacer) Estos chicos _____ su trabajo si comprendieran la tarea.

5. (escribir) Yo creía que Uds. me _____ más mensajes electrónicos.

6. (salir) Sabíamos que tú _____ con nosotros.

7. (caber) Pensábamos que la maleta _____.

8. (decir) Yo te _____ la respuesta si la supiera.

9. (vender) Si pudiéramos, _____ nuestra casa.

10. (querer) Ella nos dijo que tú _____ ir.

11. (haber) Yo no sabía si _____ una fiesta o no.

12. (dar) En ese caso yo no le _____ el dinero.

◀ *For more help, see* Conditional tenses, *page 101.*

I Answer each of the following questions to say that all this has already been done, using the present perfect tense, as in the model.

MODELO ¿Carmela va a salir? __Ya ha salido.__

1. ¿Vas a abrir las ventanas? _____

2. ¿Los chicos van a poner la mesa? _____

3. ¿Uds. van a hacer ejercicio? _____

4. ¿José va a llamar? _____

5. ¿Vas a pedir una pizza? _____

6. ¿Nosotros vamos a ver la película? _____

7. ¿Carlos y Pedro van a volver? _____

8. ¿Van Uds. a escribir el mensaje? _____

◀ *For more help, see* Present perfect tense, *page 103.*

J Answer each of the following questions, using the past perfect (pluperfect) tense and the word ya, as in the model.

MODELO ¿Ella quería cenar? __Ya había cenado.__

1. ¿Tu mamá quería salir? _____

2. ¿Tú querías hacer el té? _____

3. ¿Los niños querían jugar? _____

4. ¿Ellas querían volver? _____

5. ¿Uds. querían hablar? _____

6. ¿Querías telefonear? _____

7. ¿Ellos querían verlo? _____

8. ¿Uds. querían comer? _____

◀ *For more help, see* Past perfect (pluperfect) tense, *page 105.*

K *Respond to each of the following exclamations, using the future perfect tense to express surprise at the event, as in the model.*

MODELO ¡Se escapó el gato! _¿Cómo se habrá escapado?_

1. ¡Ellos lo supieron! _____

2. ¡Tú ganaste! _____

3. ¡Los amigos llegaron! _____

4. ¡Uds. sacaron el premio! _____

5. ¡Yo conseguí el trabajo! _____

6. ¡El niño reparó el juguete! _____

◀ *For more help, see* Future perfect tense, *page 109.*

L *Rewrite each of the following sentences in the passive voice, keeping the same tense as in the original sentence.*

1. Los niños tiran la pelota.

_____

2. Pablo escribió el mensaje.

_____

3. Los expertos han estudiado el informe.

_____

4. Todos admiran a esta cantante.

_____

5. La policía arrestó a los criminales.

_____

6. Mi abuela ha hecho la cena.

_____

7. La ciudad construirá un nuevo estadio.

_____

8. El director organizará un comité.

_____

◀ *For more help, see* Passive voice, *page 113.*

M *Complete the following chart with* tú *commands, as in the model.*

	INFINITIVE	AFFIRMATIVE COMMAND	NEGATIVE COMMAND
MODELO	llamarlo	*Llámalo.*	*No lo llames.*
1.	dármelo	_____	_____
2.	escribirle	_____	_____
3.	salir	_____	_____
4.	decírnoslo	_____	_____
5.	hacerlo	_____	_____
6.	vendérsela	_____	_____
7.	ponerlo	_____	_____

◀ *For more help, see* Imperative mood, *page 115.*

N *Complete the following chart with* Ud. *commands, as in the model.*

	INFINITIVE	AFFIRMATIVE COMMAND	NEGATIVE COMMAND
MODELO	llamarlo	*Llámelo.*	*No lo llame.*
1.	decírmelo	_____	_____
2.	abrirlas	_____	_____
3.	oírla	_____	_____
4.	verlos	_____	_____
5.	hacerlo	_____	_____
6.	aprenderlos	_____	_____
7.	conocerlo	_____	_____

◀ *For more help, see* Imperative mood, *page 115.*

O *Complete the following sentences with the correct present subjunctive or present indicative form of the verb in parentheses.*

1. (poder) Es poco probable que él _____ venir.

2. (entender) No creo que ella _____ lo que le dices.

3. (querer) Sé que los chicos _____ acompañarnos.

4. (saber) Me sorprende que tú no _____ la respuesta.

5. (escoger) Él teme que yo no lo _____.

6. (ir) Estamos contentos que Uds. _____ a España.

7. (volver) Estamos seguros de que él _____ mañana.

8. (hacer) Es mejor que yo _____ este trabajo.

9. (conocer) Mamá quiere que nosotros _____ a los invitados.

10. (seguir)   Es importante que tú _____ mis consejos.

11. (ver)   Queremos que los niños _____ esta película.

12. (estar)   Espero que todos Uds. _____ bien.

13. (venir)   Me alegro de que Uds. _____ a vernos.

14. (dar)   Es necesario que ella se _____ cuenta de esto.

15. (pedir)   Él no quiere que nosotros se lo _____ otra vez.

◀ *For more help, see* Subjunctive mood, *pages 117 and 119–121.*

P *Complete each of the following sentences with the correct imperfect subjunctive form of the verb in parentheses.*

1. (hacer)   Quería que Uds. lo _____.

2. (saber)   No creíamos que Ud. lo _____.

3. (prestar)   Era necesario que tú me lo _____.

4. (ser)   Esperaba que la casa _____ más moderna.

5. (pasar)   Queríamos que Uds. _____ por nosotros.

6. (ir)   Le pedí que _____ conmigo.

7. (recoger)   Les mandé que _____ todos los papeles.

8. (decir)   Insistieron en que yo se lo _____ todo.

9. (traducir)   Me sorprendía que nadie _____ el discurso del presidente.

10. (hablar)   Prefería que tú me _____ en español.

11. (dar)   Le dije que venías para que te _____ el paquete.

12. (volver)   Le avisé antes de que él _____.

◀ *For more help, see* Imperfect subjunctive, *page 121.*

Q *Complete each of the following sentences with the correct forms of the verbs in parentheses. Use the pluperfect subjunctive in the if-clause and the conditional perfect in the main clause.*

1. Si nosotros lo _____ (saber),

   _____ (venir).

2. Ella te _____ (ayudar) si tú se lo

   _____ (pedir).

3. Él no _____ (decírselo) si ella

   _____ (estar) informada.

4. Yo no _____ (hacerlo) si alguien

   _____ (decirme) que se prohibía.

5. Si tú _____ (poner) atención, tú

   _____ (sacar) mejores notas.

6. Si ellos _____ (estudiar),

   _____ (salir) bien en los exámenes.

7. Si yo _____ (estar) lista, yo

   _____ (poder) salir con ellos.

8. Tú _____ (comprender) si tú

   _____ (esforzarse) un poco.

◀ *For more help, see* Past perfect (pluperfect) subjunctive, *page 123;* Conditional perfect tense, *page 111.*

Using your Spanish

Now that you have practiced the mechanics of Spanish, you can use your knowledge to express yourself in meaningful contextual exercises. Each exercise below shows you how to apply one or more grammatical elements in everyday situations. A cross-reference to the relevant grammar points discussed in this book is provided at the end of each exercise. An answer key is provided after the appendices.

A Dinner is ready.

Sergio Torres, head chef of the catering company Comilón, asks his employees if they are going to do certain things to prepare and serve the dinner. They tell him that they did these things already. To express this, write sentences using the preterite, changing direct object nouns to pronouns, as in the model.

MODELO   Arturo, ¿vas a leer la receta de cocina? ___Ya la leí.___

1. Antonio, ¿vas a preparar el pescado? _____

2. Gloria, ¿vas a sacar los platos? _____

3. Pilar y Jorge, ¿van a arreglar las flores? _____

4. Iván y Lucía, ¿van a poner la mesa? _____

5. Carlota, ¿vas a hacer los pasteles? _____

6. Fernanda, ¿vas a servir la sopa? _____

7. Mario y Roberto, ¿van a abrir las botellas de vino? _____

8. Pablo, ¿vas a cortar el pan? _____

◀ *For more help, see* Preterite tense, *page 97;* Personal pronouns, *pages 23 and 25.*

B Summer plans

You and your friends are discussing your summer plans. To tell what each person wants or plans to do, combine each group of elements into a complete sentence, as in the model. In each case, determine which preposition, if any, is used before the infinitive. Use the present tense.

MODELO   Marco/desear/pasar un mes en Madrid

   Marco desea pasar un mes en Madrid.

1. David/comenzar/tomar un curso de chino en línea

   _____

2. Claudia y Leonardo/querer/recorrer Europa

   _____

3. yo/pensar/leer todas la obras de Shakespeare

   _____

4. Viviana/ir/ser voluntaria en un hospital de niños

   _____

5. tú y yo/tratar/encontrar trabajo en una empresa multinacional

   _____

6. Sofía/soñar/ser actriz en Hollywood

   _____

7. tú/esperar/perfeccionar tu español

   _____

8. Uds./preferir/relajarse en la playa

   _____

9. Timoteo/interesarse/participar en una excavación arqueológica (*archaeological dig*)

   _____

◀ *For more help, see* Present tense, *pages 91–93;* Introducing prepositions, *pages 75–77;* Present infinitives, *page 85.*

C Events and backgrounds: What was the weather like?

To tell about Samuel and Sara Herrera's trip, combine each group of elements into a complete sentence, as in the model. Describe what the weather was like for each situation. In each sentence, use the imperfect to describe the background action, and use the preterite for the event itself. Note that weather, time, and feelings are usually background actions in past time, not events. Use cuando (*"when"*) *to connect the clauses.*

MODELO   hacer sol/Samuel y Sara/salir de la casa

   Hacía sol cuando Samuel y Sara salieron de la casa.

1. estar nublado/ellos/llegar al aeropuerto

   _____

2. llover/el avión/despegar

_____

3. estar despejado/el avión/aterrizar

_____

4. hacer buen tiempo/Sara y Samuel/registrarse (*check in*) en el hotel

_____

5. hacer mucho calor en la habitación/Samuel/prender el aire acondicionado

_____

6. lloviznar (*drizzle*)/Samuel y Sara/comenzar a hacer turismo

_____

7. haber truenos y relámpagos (*thunder and lightning*)/Sara y Samuel/entrar en el teatro

_____

◄ *For more help, see* Preterite tense, *page 97;* Imperfect tense, *page 95.*

D More events and backgrounds: What time was it?

To tell at what time Camila and her family did things in their daily routine, combine each group of elements into a complete sentence, as in the model. In each sentence, use the imperfect to describe the background action, and use the preterite for the event itself. Note that weather, time, and feelings are usually background actions in past time, not events. Use cuando *("when") to connect the clauses.*

MODELO   ser las siete/Camila/despertarse

   Eran las siete cuando Camila se despertó.

1. ser las ocho/tú/limpiarse los dientes

_____

2. ser las diez y media/sus hermanas/vestirse

_____

3. ser las once/Teresa y yo/pintarse los labios

_____

4. ser la una en punto/Fernando/ducharse

_____

5. ser las tres y cuarto/yo/secarse el pelo

_____

6. ser las cinco/Arturo y Mariano/afeitarse

_____

7. ser las seis y media/su hermano/ponerse los zapatos

_____

8. ser medianoche/sus papás/acostarse

_____

◄ *For more help, see* Reflexive/reciprocal pronouns, *page 31;* Preterite tense, *page 97;* Imperfect tense, *page 95.*

E   What was the question?

Felipe is talking to someone on his cell phone. Daniel hears only what Felipe is answering, but he can't hear the questions. Write the questions Daniel would have asked to elicit Felipe's responses. Use the tú *form, and choose* ser *or* estar *in forming your questions.*

MODELO   <u>¿Dónde estás?</u>

¿Yo? En el centro comercial.

1. _____

¿Nosotros? Con Gregorio y Elena.

2. _____

¿El restaurante mexicano? A la vuelta de la esquina.

3. _____

¿La hora? Casi las cinco.

4. _____

¿Camilo y Carmen? Emocionados.

5. _____

¿El reloj? De oro.

6. _____

¿El iPod? Para mi esposa.

7. _____

¿Los nuevos programadores? Inteligentes.

8. _____

¿La familia de Isabel? De origen español.

9. _____

¿Yo? Acatarrado.

10. _____

¿Mis papás? De viaje.

11. _____

¿La reunión? En la sala de conferencias (*conference room*).

◄ *For more help, see* Uses of *ser* and *estar, pages 175–176;* Introducing questions, *page 83.*

F Asking for advice

Carmen asks Mariana if she should do certain things. Mariana tells her to do them, responding with an affirmative tú *command. Write Mariana's response, changing direct object nouns to pronouns and making all necessary changes, as in the model.*

MODELO ¿Debo enseñarle la casa a Ana? __Sí, enséñasela.__

1. ¿Debo mandarle las fotos a Carlos? _____

2. ¿Debo prestarle la computadora a Juana? _____

3. ¿Debo entregarles los datos a los analistas? _____

4. ¿Debo traerle los disquetes a Miguel? _____

5. ¿Debo darle el dinero al contador? _____

6. ¿Debo pedirle el carro a María Teresa? _____

7. ¿Debo servirles las manzanas a los niños? _____

8. ¿Debo regalarle la cámara a mi hermana? _____

◀ *For more help, see* Imperative mood, *page 115;* Personal pronouns, *pages 25 and 27.*

G How was the party?

Rebeca could not attend Carolina's surprise birthday party and asks Anita how it was. To find out what Anita said, write a response to each question, changing the adjectives in parentheses to adverbs ending in -mente, as in the model.

MODELO ¿Cómo habló Marisol? (caluroso)

__Habló calurosamente.__

1. ¿Cómo bailaron Rafael y Beatriz? (elegante)

_____

2. ¿Cómo se expresó Paloma? (amable)

_____

3. ¿Cómo tocó el piano Alejandro? (artístico)

_____

4. ¿Cómo presentaron su regalo los señores Fuentes? (generoso)

_____

5. ¿Cómo cantó Victoria? (hermoso)

_____

6. ¿Cómo sirvieron la comida? (lujoso)

_____

7. ¿Cómo reaccionó Carolina? (feliz)

_____

◀ *For more help, see* Introducing adverbs, *page 61.*

H He can't find anything!

Rodrigo and Jimena Salazar are about to leave on a trip. As usual, Rodrigo can't find things. Create dialogues between them about all the things Rodrigo can't find, using the present, future, and imperative tenses. Use the tú *form, and change direct object nouns to pronouns, as in the model.*

MODELO   ¿Dónde están las llaves?

       RODRIGO   ¿Dónde están las llaves? __No las encuentro.__

       JIMENA   __Mi amor, búscalas. Las encontrarás.__

1. RODRIGO   ¿Dónde está mi cartera? _____

    JIMENA   _____

2. RODRIGO   ¿Dónde está mi pasaporte? _____

    JIMENA   _____

3. RODRIGO   ¿Dónde están las cámaras? _____

    JIMENA   _____

4. RODRIGO   ¿Dónde están los maletines? _____

    JIMENA   _____

5. RODRIGO   ¿Dónde está el plano de la ciudad? _____

    JIMENA   _____

6. RODRIGO   ¿Dónde están los billetes de avión? _____

    JIMENA   _____

7. RODRIGO   ¿Dónde está mi cartapacio (*briefcase*)? _____

    JIMENA   _____

8. RODRIGO   ¿Dónde están los mapas? _____

    JIMENA   _____

9. RODRIGO   ¿Dónde está mi teléfono celular? _____

    JIMENA   _____

10. RODRIGO   ¿Dónde están mis tarjetas de crédito? _____

    JIMENA   _____

◀ *For more help, see* Personal pronouns, *pages 23, 25, and 27;* Present tense, *pages 91–93;* Future tense, *page 99;* Imperative mood, *page 115.*

I Where are they from?

Alejandro and Miguel are discussing the nationalities of their business school colleagues. Write Miguel's response to Alejandro's assumptions about where each person is from, as in the model. Derive adjectives of nationality from the countries named in the question and the cue in parentheses.

MODELO   ALEJANDRO   Roberto es de México, ¿verdad? (Perú)

           MIGUEL   *No, no es mexicano. Es peruano.*

1. ALEJANDRO   Elena es de Inglaterra, ¿verdad? (Escocia)

   MIGUEL   _____

2. ALEJANDRO   Gerardo y Paula son de Chile, ¿verdad? (Costa Rica)

   MIGUEL   _____

3. ALEJANDRO   Esteban es de Italia, ¿verdad? (Francia)

   MIGUEL   _____

4. ALEJANDRO   Los señores Suárez son de España, ¿verdad? (Puerto Rico)

   MIGUEL   _____

5. ALEJANDRO   El primo de Guillermo es de Brasil, ¿verdad? (Portugal)

   MIGUEL   _____

6. ALEJANDRO   David es de Israel, ¿verdad? (Estados Unidos)

   MIGUEL   _____

7. ALEJANDRO   Ricardo y Margarita son de Canadá, ¿verdad? (India)

   MIGUEL   _____

8. ALEJANDRO   Sus amigas son de China, ¿verdad? (Japón)

   MIGUEL   _____

9. ALEJANDRO   Tú [masc.] eres de Rusia, ¿verdad? (Alemania)

   MIGUEL   _____

10. ALEJANDRO   Uds. [masc.] son de Colombia, ¿verdad? (Venezuela)

    MIGUEL   _____

◀ *For more help, see* Descriptive adjectives, *pages 46–47;* Uses of *ser* and *estar,* *pages 175–176;* Introducing adverbs, *page 63.*

J No, they're the same.

Luisa and Emilia are comparing people and things. Luisa says someone or something is more _____ than someone or something else. Emilia disagrees, suggesting they are equally _____. Combine each group of elements into a complete sentence by Luisa, which Emilia contradicts, as in the model. Make sure that adjectives agree with the nouns they modify.

MODELO Jaime/gracioso/Ramón

    LUISA   *Jaime es más gracioso que Ramón.*

    EMILIA   *¡Qué va! Ramón es tan gracioso como Jaime.*

1. Sofía/encantador/Mateo

    LUISA   _____

    EMILIA   _____

2. las películas/divertido/las obras de teatro

    LUISA   _____

    EMILIA   _____

3. la señorita Rivera/cortés/el señor Peña

    LUISA   _____

    EMILIA   _____

4. la tienda de ropa/elegante/la tienda por departamentos

    LUISA   _____

    EMILIA   _____

5. estos novelistas/célebre/esos poetas

    LUISA   _____

    EMILIA   _____

6. Pedro/simpático/Carlota

    LUISA   _____

    EMILIA   _____

7. los ingenieros/trabajador/los arquitectos

    LUISA   _____

    EMILIA   _____

8. las tortas/dulce/los pasteles

    LUISA   _____

    EMILIA   _____

9. aquel condominio/caro/esta casa

    LUISA   _____

    EMILIA   _____

10. Benjamín y Raquel/talentoso/Rebeca y Aurora

    LUISA   _____

    EMILIA   _____

◀ *For more help, see* Comparison of adjectives, *pages 48–49.*

K A musical family

Complete this story about a family of musicians by filling in each blank with the correct definite or indefinite article. Place an X in the space if no article is needed.

_____ (1) familia Mondragón es célebre en _____ (2) mundo de _____ (3) música. Lorenzo, _____ (4) cantante de ópera, es _____ (5) gran artista. Su esposa, Isabel, es _____ (6) artista muy conocida también. Toca _____ (7) violín en _____ (8) de _____ (9) orquestas más importantes de _____ (10) país. _____ (11) dos hijos de _____ (12) señores Mondragón también se dedican a _____ (13) música. Diego es _____ (14) director de orquesta y su hermana Susana es _____ (15) compositora muy talentosa.

◀ *For more help, see* Introducing determiners, *pages 17–18.*

L The chores? We've already done them.

Regina counts on her friends to help her with household chores. She gives them orders, but they respond that they have already done the chores. Combine each group of elements to create a dialogue, using affirmative Uds. *commands in the first line and the present perfect tense in the response, as in the model. Change direct object nouns to pronouns in the responses.*

MODELO   Jorge y Nicolás/pasar la aspiradora

REGINA   _Jorge y Nicolás, pasen la aspiradora._

JORGE Y NICOLÁS   _Ya la hemos pasado._

1. Mario y Benita/reciclar los periódicos

   REGINA   _____

   MARIO Y BENITA   _____

2. Clara y Carmen/poner la mesa

   REGINA   _____

   CLARA Y CARMEN   _____

3. Antonio y Arón/cortar el césped (*grass*)

   REGINA   _____

   ANTONIO Y ARÓN   _____

4. Maite y Eva/hacer el almuerzo

   REGINA   _____

   MAITE Y EVA   _____

5. Andrés y Araceli/sacar la basura

   REGINA   _____

   ANDRÉS Y ARACELI   _____

6. Victoria y Javier/correr los muebles

REGINA _____

VICTORIA Y JAVIER _____

7. Lupe y Felipe/pasear al perro

REGINA _____

LUPE Y FELIPE _____

8. Alfonso y Luis/colgar los cuadros

REGINA _____

ALFONSO Y LUIS _____

◀ *For more help, see* Imperative mood, *page 115;* Present perfect tense, *pages 103 and 105;* Personal pronouns, *pages 23 and 25.*

M Everyone is busy.

Juan José would like to play tennis right now, but everyone is too busy to join him. To tell what they are doing, combine each group of elements into a complete sentence, using the present progressive, as in the model. Attach reflexive pronouns to the present participle for reflexive verbs.

MODELO mis amigos/jugar al golf

Mis amigos están jugando al golf.

1. Alberto/navegar en la Red

_____

2. tú/enviar e-mails

_____

3. mi hermano/oír música

_____

4. Leonor/lavarse el pelo

_____

5. Timoteo/tomar un café en un cibercafé

_____

6. mis primas/leer unas novelas policíacas

_____

7. Uds./ver las noticias

_____

8. Gerardo/vestirse para salir con su novia

_____

◀ *For more help, see* Present tense, *page 91;* Personal pronouns, *page 27.*

N Whose is it?

Paloma wonders to whom some items belong and asks her friend Eva about them. Eva says they do not belong to the people asked about. Combine each group of elements to create a dialogue between Paloma and Eva, as in the model. Use demonstrative adjectives for the items in the questions and long-form possessive adjectives in the responses.

MODELO   sombrero/Alfredo

PALOMA   *¿Este sombrero es de Alfredo?*

EVA   *No, no es suyo.*

1. abrigos/Mateo y Gabriela

PALOMA _____

EVA _____

2. bolsa/Juana

PALOMA _____

EVA _____

3. pulseras/las hermanas Castillo

PALOMA _____

EVA _____

4. gorro/Moisés

PALOMA _____

EVA _____

5. pendientes/Sandra

PALOMA _____

EVA _____

6. guantes/el señor Soto

PALOMA _____

EVA _____

7. sortija/tu amiga

PALOMA _____

EVA _____

8. gafas de sol/María Rosa

PALOMA _____

EVA _____

9. paraguas/profesor Sánchez

PALOMA _____

EVA _____

10. billetero/tu padre

PALOMA _____

EVA _____

11. suéteres/los gemelos (*twins*)

PALOMA _____

EVA _____

◀ *For more help, see* Demonstrative adjectives, *page 51;* Possessive adjectives, *page 53.*

O   Attitudes and opinions

Tell what people think about each event. Complete each sentence, using either the present indicative or the present subjunctive in the subordinate clause, as in the model.

MODELO   Me dices la verdad.

    a. Yo necesito ___*que me digas la verdad*___.

    b. Yo pienso ___*que me dices la verdad*___.

1. Manolo y Celeste se gradúan en junio.

    a. Yo creo _____.

    b. Es bueno _____.

    c. Sabemos _____.

2. Esteban viene a vernos el sábado.

    a. Es cierto _____.

    b. Prefiero _____.

    c. Dudamos _____.

3. Uds. tienen mucho éxito con su empresa.

    a. Todos quieren _____.

    b. Me alegro _____.

    c. Ojalá _____.

4. Nora y Osvaldo van a casarse en enero.

    a. Sus papás insisten _____.

    b. Nos parece _____.

    c. Todos están contentísimos _____.

5. Hay problemas con la base de datos.

    a. Es verdad _____.

    b. Niegan _____.

    c. Nos sorprende _____.

6. Llueve el día de la excursión.

    a. Sienten _____.

    b. Se ve _____.

    c. Temen _____.

7. Adriana es atenta y responsable.

    a. Es necesario _____.

    b. Exigimos _____.

    c. No es verdad _____.

◀ *For more help, see* Subjunctive mood, *pages 117 and 119–120.*

P   The first day of class

Señorita Cepeda's students have many questions about the class. Combine each group of elements to write conversational exchanges between la maestra *and her students, as in the model. Use the future tense for questions asked by the students and the present subjunctive for the teacher's responses.*

MODELO   (Pablo) nosotros/estudiar mucho : maestra/es necesario

       PABLO   _Señorita, ¿tendremos que estudiar mucho?_

       SEÑORITA   _Sí, Pablo, es necesario que estudien mucho._

1. (Débora) nosotros/llegar a las ocho en punto : maestra/insisto en

    DÉBORA   _____

    SEÑORITA   _____

2. (Maximiliano) nosotros/comprar siete libros de texto : maestra/quiero

    MAXIMILIANO   _____

    SEÑORITA   _____

3. (Carmencita) nosotros/hacer la tarea todos los días : maestra/les exijo

    CARMENCITA   _____

    SEÑORITA   _____

4. (Miguelito) nosotros/aprender todas las fechas de memoria : maestra/es importante

    MIGUELITO   _____

    SEÑORITA   _____

5. (Pepe) nosotros/leer varios capítulos todos los días : maestra/espero

    PEPE   _____

    SEÑORITA   _____

6. (Inés) nosotros/traer la calculadora de bolsillo : maestra/necesito

    INÉS   _____

    SEÑORITA   _____

7. (Paquito) nosotros/escribir composiciones : maestra/es bueno

PAQUITO   _____

SEÑORITA   _____

◀ For more help, see Subjunctive mood, *pages 117 and 119–120*; Future tense, *page 99*.

Q   Friends

These people like each other and get on very well. Combine each group of elements to write sentences describing their relationships, as in the model. Use the reflexive pronoun with verbs to convey reciprocal meaning ("each other").

MODELO   Gerardo y Alana/verse todos los días

      Gerardo y Alana se ven todos los días.

1. Roberto y Leonardo/hablar por celular

_____

2. Marisol y César/entender bien

_____

3. Ud. y yo/conocer bien

_____

4. Marta y Moisés/querer

_____

5. Diana y Rosa/ayudar mucho

_____

6. tú y yo/tutear (*address each other as* tú [informally])

_____

7. Paco y María/comprar regalos

_____

8. Octavio y yo/escribir muchos correos electrónicos

_____

◀ For more help, see Reflexive/reciprocal pronouns, *page 31*.

R   Problems and solutions

Combine each group of elements to propose a solution for each of the stated problems, as in the model. Use double object pronouns in your responses.

MODELO   Ricardo no sabe el número de teléfono de Julián. (yo/ir a/decir)

      Yo voy a decírselo.

1. Emilia quiere ver el nuevo museo de arte. (nosotros/deber/enseñar)

_____

2. Mercedes y Julio quieren probar los tacos. (tú/poder/servir)

_____

3. Joselito no sabe leer este libro. (hay que/leer)

_____

4. El jefe necesita el informe hoy. (yo/pensar/entregar)

_____

5. Los profesores insisten en saber la verdad. (Uds./deber/contar)

_____

6. Tú quieres usar nuestras maletas. (nosotros/poder/prestar)

_____

7. Sus colegas no entienden la idea. (Ud./ir a/explicar)

_____

8. Tú quieres oír los discos compactos. (ellos/pensar/traer)

_____

◀ *For more help, see* Personal pronouns, *pages 23, 25, and 27;* Introducing prepositions, *pages 75–77.*

S   Conversation

Claudia is asking Pilar about her date with Juan Carlos yesterday. Write the question that Claudia would have asked to elicit each of Pilar's responses, as in the model. Focus on the words in italics.

MODELO   CLAUDIA   <u>¿En quién piensas?</u>

            PILAR   Yo pienso en *Juan Carlos*.

1. CLAUDIA   _____

    PILAR   Yo fui *al café Sevilla* ayer.

2. CLAUDIA   _____

    PILAR   Salí con *Juan Carlos*.

3. CLAUDIA   _____

    PILAR   Nos encontramos *a las cuatro de la tarde*.

4. CLAUDIA   _____

    PILAR   Yo tomé *un café con leche* y él tomó *un expreso*.

5. CLAUDIA   _____

    PILAR   De postre pedimos *una tarta de limón*.

_____

6. CLAUDIA   _____

   PILAR   Hablamos *del trabajo, de la familia, de muchas cosas.*

7. CLAUDIA   _____

   PILAR   No cenamos juntos porque *yo tenía que terminar mi informe.*

8. CLAUDIA   _____

   PILAR   Quedamos en vernos *el viernes.*

◀ *For more help, see* Introducing questions, *page 83;* Interrogative pronouns, *pages 41–42;* Interrogative adjectives, *page 55;* Comparison of interrogative pronouns and interrogative adjectives, *page 172.*

T   In the department store

Leonor asks for Luisa's advice as she shops for clothing for her husband. Write a response, as in the models, using the demonstrative pronouns given as cues.

MODELOS   ¿Te gusta este abrigo? (ese)   <u>Sí, pero me gusta más ése.</u>

          ¿Te gustan estos abrigos? (ese) <u>Sí, pero me gustan más ésos.</u>

1. ¿Te gusta esa camisa? (este)   _____

2. ¿Te gustan estos zapatos? (aquel)   _____

3. ¿Te gustan aquellos trajes? (ese)   _____

4. ¿Te gusta este cinturón? (ese)   _____

5. ¿Te gustan esos pantalones? (este)   _____

6. ¿Te gusta esta corbata? (aquel)   _____

7. ¿Te gustan aquellas medias? (ese)   _____

8. ¿Te gusta ese smoking (*tuxedo*)? (este)   _____

◀ *For more help, see* Personal pronouns, *page 25;* Demonstrative pronouns, *page 39.*

U   Likes

To tell what people like, combine each group of elements into a complete sentence, as in the model.

MODELO   (a él)/gustar/el chocolate

      <u>Le gusta el chocolate.</u>

1. a mí/gustar/la música clásica

   _____

2. (a Uds.)/gustar/el fútbol

   _____

3. (a ti)/gustar/los animales

   _____

4. (a ellas)/gustar/el cine inglés

_____

5. (a nosotros)/gustar/las ciencias naturales

_____

6. (a ella)/gustar/la comida italiana

_____

7. (a él)/gustar/los deportes

_____

8. (a Ud.)/gustar/los bombones artesanos

_____

◀ *For more help, see* Personal pronouns, *page 25.*

V If it were possible . . .

*Susana and her friends are thinking about the things they would do if they could.
To find out what they're thinking, complete each of the following sentences with the
correct form of the verbs in parentheses. Use the imperfect subjunctive in the if-clause
and the conditional tense in the main clause, as in the model.*

MODELO   Si ___*fuera*___ (ser) posible, yo ___*viajaría*___ (viajar) todo el año.

1. Si Bernardo no _____ (trabajar) en el centro,

   _____ (vivir) en el campo.

2. Julieta y Jaime _____ (mudarse) si _____ (encontrar)
   una casa asequible (*affordable*).

3. Si tú no _____ (tener) que trabajar, _____ (ser)
   muy feliz.

4. Judit y yo _____ (asistir) al concierto esta noche si

   _____ (poder) conseguir billetes.

5. Si Uds. _____ (ganar) más dinero, _____ (poder)
   ahorrar más.

6. Todos nosotros _____ (ir) a la costa si _____ (hacer)
   buen tiempo.

7. Si Consuelo _____ (ir) a Chile, _____ (ver)
   a sus tíos.

8. Si _____ (haber) una exposición de arte neoclásico en el museo,

   Ud. _____ (querer) verla.

9. Yo _____ (hacer) un plan de negocios si ellos me lo

   _____ (pedir).

10. Nosotros _____ (salir) a divertirnos si tú

 _____ (venir) a verme.

11. Pablo y Carmen _____ (ponerse) en contacto contigo si tú les

 _____ (dar) tu dirección electrónica.

12. Si nosotros _____ (estar) de vacaciones, _____
(estar) muy contentos.

◀ *For more help, see* Conditional tenses, *page 101;* Imperfect subjunctive, *page 121.*

W   Situations

Tell what people would do in the following situations. Write a sentence expressing a solution to the problem, using the cues given, as in the models. Use the conditional tense of the verb.

MODELOS   Está lloviendo muy fuerte. Tienes que ir a la universidad. ¿Qué harías?

     a. ir en coche

       Iría en coche.

     b. usar el paraguas

       Usaría el paraguas.

1. Mario quiere tomar un café antes de ir a la oficina. Se le acabó (*he ran out of*) el café. ¿Qué haría él?

     a. comprar café en el supermercado

     b. tomar un café en Starbucks camino a (*en route to*) la oficina

2. Los empleados tienen que imprimir unos documentos. La impresora está descompuesta. ¿Qué harían?

     a. llamar al técnico

     b. repararla ellos mismos

3. Raquel trabajó muchísimo hoy. Está cansadísima, completamente agotada. ¿Qué haría?

     a. acostarse al llegar a la casa

     b. salir a divertirse con sus amigos

4. Jaime cree algo que no es cierto. Todos le dicen mentiras. ¿Qué harías tú?

   a. decirle la verdad

   _____

   b. mentirle también

   _____

5. La novia de Felipe es celosa y gruñona (*grumpy*), pero Felipe sigue con ella. ¿Qué harían Uds.?

   a. romper con ella

   _____

   b. tratar de cambiarla

   _____

6. Celeste recibió una fuerte cantidad de dinero. Quiere darles el dinero a sus papás. ¿Qué harían sus amigos?

   a. invertir el dinero

   _____

   b. donar el dinero a instituciones caritativas (*charitable*)

   _____

7. Joselito está acatarrado. Sus papás quieren llevarlo al pediatra. ¿Qué haría su abuela?

   a. prepararle una sopa de pollo

   _____

   b. tomarle la temperatura

   _____

8. Ud. hizo una cena para varios invitados. Toda la comida salió mal. ¿Qué harías?

   a. servir la comida pidiendo disculpas

   _____

   b. sacar a los invitados a cenar en un restaurante

   _____

◀ *For more help, see* Conditional tenses, *page 101.*

X Let's do it. No, let's not.

Simón suggests things that he and his friends can do. Some want to do these things, others do not. To express the friends' responses, write sentences, using affirmative and negative nosotros *commands, as in the model.*

MODELO SIMÓN   —¿Por qué no trotamos?

   ROBERTO   —Sí, vamos a trotar.

   LIDIA   —No, no trotemos.

1. SIMÓN   ¿Por qué no hacemos una fiesta?

JORGE   _____

TERESA   _____

2. SIMÓN   ¿Por qué no salimos a una discoteca?

MARÍA ELENA   _____

CRISTÓBAL   _____

3. SIMÓN   ¿Por qué no navegamos en la Red?

FLOR   _____

ALICIA   _____

4. SIMÓN   ¿Por qué no jugamos al béisbol?

DIEGO   _____

PACO   _____

5. SIMÓN   ¿Por qué no comemos una pizza?

DIANA   _____

TOMÁS   _____

6. SIMÓN   ¿Por qué no vemos una película?

CARMEN   _____

RAFA   _____

7. SIMÓN   ¿Por qué no vamos a un concierto?

LUCERO   _____

GRACIELA   _____

8. SIMÓN   ¿Por qué no oímos música?

VERÓNICA   _____

CLAUDIO   _____

◀ *For more help, see* Imperative mood, *page 115.*

Y   Growing our business

Teodoro García and Esteban Vargas describe the personnel they need to grow their business. To find out what their needs are, combine each pair of sentences into a single sentence, as in the model. Use a subordinate adjective clause in the present subjunctive.

MODELO   Necesitamos un secretario. Él debe ser bilingüe.

     Necesitamos un secretario que sea bilingüe.

1. Buscamos un director ejecutivo. Él debe definir estrategia para la empresa.

_____

2. Queremos programadores. Ellos deben conocer los lenguajes y sistemas a fondo.

_____

3. Necesito asesores. Ellos deben encontrar soluciones a los problemas de sus clientes.

_____

4. Quieren un especialista en marketing. Él debe saber analizar los productos desde el punto de vista del consumidor.

_____

_____

5. Buscan un director de finanzas. Él debe dirigir eficazmente las operaciones financieras de la empresa.

_____

_____

6. Necesitamos vendedores. Deben poder viajar a menudo.

_____

7. Busco un diseñador. Debe crear sitios web llamativos (*striking*).

_____

8. Quiero un abogado. Él debe tener profundos conocimientos del derecho comercial.

_____

◀ *For more help, see* Subjunctive mood, *pages 117 and 119–120;* Relative pronouns, *page 35.*

Z   A better vacation

To express what Lorenzo and Olivia Ramírez should have or should not have done to make their vacation more enjoyable, write sentences consisting of a main clause in the conditional perfect and an if-clause in the pluperfect subjunctive, as in the model.

MODELO   Nosotros fuimos de vacaciones en agosto. Hacía mucho calor.

Si no hubiéramos ido de vacaciones en agosto, no habría

hecho tanto calor.

1. Fuimos a la playa. Lo pasamos mal.

_____

2. El hotel estaba sucio. No estábamos a gusto.

_____

3. Los restaurantes eran malos. Uds. se enfermaron.

_____

4. Llovió todos los días. No nadamos.

_____

5. El cine estaba cerrado. No vimos una película.

   _____

6. No me eché repelente contra los insectos. Los mosquitos me picaron.

   _____

7. Nuestros amigos no nos acompañaron. No nos divertimos.

   _____

8. Nos quedamos en la playa dos semanas. Nos aburrimos.

   _____

◀ *For more help, see* Conditional perfect tense, *page 111;* Past perfect (pluperfect) subjunctive, *page 123;* Reflexive/reciprocal pronouns, *page 31.*

AA Reactions

Describe how people react to certain statements about past occurrences. Write sentences using the cue in the main clause and either the present perfect subjunctive or the present perfect in the subordinate clause, as in the model.

MODELO   Uds. no vieron el programa.

     a. No pienso ___que Uds. hayan visto el programa___.

     b. Es obvio ___que Uds. no han visto el programa___.

1. Gonzalo y Érica regresaron de su luna de miel (*honeymoon*).

   a. No creemos _____.

   b. Me parece _____.

2. Le dijiste lo que pasó.

   a. Piensan _____.

   b. Es mejor _____.

3. El perro de Elián murió.

   a. Sienten _____.

   b. Sabemos _____.

4. Santiago se puso gordo.

   a. Creen _____.

   b. Es malo _____.

5. Uds. no se aprovecharon de esta oportunidad.

   a. Es una lástima _____.

   b. Es cierto _____.

6. Mercedes y Javier rompieron su compromiso.

   a. Me sorprende _____.

   b. Se ve _____.

7. Joaquín invirtió dinero en la Bolsa.

   a. Es bueno _____.

   b. Dudo _____.

8. Ud. no oyó la mala noticia.

   a. Es mejor _____.

   b. Esperamos _____.

9. Hicimos una excursión.

   a. No es verdad _____.

   b. Me alegro _____.

10. Les devolvieron el dinero.

   a. Es dudoso _____.

   b. No es cierto _____.

◀ *For more help, see* Present perfect tense, *pages 103 and 105;* Past perfect (pluperfect) subjunctive, *page 123.*

BB Going negative

Antonia is very unpleasant and says "no" to everything. Answer the questions as Antonia would, using negative words and expressions that correspond to the affirmative ones in the questions, as in the model. Retain the tense of the question in your response.

MODELO ¿Quieres comer algo? ___No, no quiero comer nada.___

1. ¿Hablaste con alguien?   _____

2. ¿Siempre vas a ese centro comercial?   _____

3. ¿Hiciste algo hoy?   _____

4. ¿Conociste a Aarón también?   _____

5. ¿Todavía estudias aeronáutica?   _____

6. ¿Buscabas a Valeria por algún lado?   _____

7. ¿Has visto a alguno de los profesores?   _____

8. ¿Fuiste alguna vez a Perú?   _____

9. ¿Manolo o Isabel te llamó?   _____

◀ *For more help, see* Introducing adverbs, *page 63.*

CC Be specific.

Julio asks Mercedes to be more specific about the things she mentions. To specify what Mercedes is talking about, write sentences that have relative clauses introduced by que, *as in the model. Use the cues in parentheses.*

MODELO ¿De qué café hablas? (Tiene buenos sándwiches.)

   ___Hablo del café que tiene buenos sándwiches.___

1. ¿De qué edificio hablas? (Queda en la calle Castaño.)

   _____

2. ¿De qué profesores hablas? (Enseñan historia inglesa.)

   _____

3. ¿De qué libro hablas? (Lo leí el mes pasado.)

   _____

4. ¿De qué tiendas de ropa hablas? (Tiene diseños de alta costura [*haute couture*].)

   _____

5. ¿De qué marca (*brand*) hablas? (Es la marca más conocida del mundo.)

   _____

6. ¿De qué restaurantes hablas? (Fueron abiertos por Franco Madero.)

   _____

7. ¿De qué flores hablas? (Me las compró Ernesto.)

   _____

8. ¿De qué documental hablas? (Se estrenó [*It premiered*] en el canal [*channel*] siete anoche.)

   _____

◀ *For more help, see* Relative pronouns, *page 35.*

DD It had already happened.

To explain what had already happened when other events occurred, combine each group of elements into a complete sentence, as in the model. Use the preterite in the subordinate clause and the past perfect tense in the main clause, and add ya *to the main clause.*

MODELO Julio/regresar a la casa : nosotros/salir

   Cuando Julio regresó a la casa, nosotros ya habíamos salido.

1. Mateo y Sofía/decidir ver la película : tú/verla

   _____

2. yo/llamar a Brígida : ella/acostarse

   _____

3. Andrés y yo/llegar al estadio de béisbol : el partido/comenzar

   _____

4. tú/venir a la oficina : la reunión/terminar

   _____

5. Uds./sentarse a la mesa : el mesero/servir el primer plato

   _____

6. Luz/levantarse : nosotros/desayunar

_____

7. Ud./encender su computadora : ellos/apagar la suya

_____

8. Javier/solicitar el puesto : los jefes/contratar a otro ingeniero

_____

9. Juan José/dejar la propina : Mauricio/pagar la cuenta

_____

10. Rebeca y Clara/entrar en la estación : su tren/partir

_____

◀ *For more help, see* Past perfect (pluperfect) tense, *page 105;* Preterite tense, *page 97.*

EE Probably

Lucía is not sure about things. To express her uncertainty, write sentences in the future tense, eliminating the italicized word or words that suggest probability.

MODELO *Probablemente* están de vacaciones. ___Estarán de vacaciones.___

1. *Supongo que* ellas tienen prisa. _____

2. *Probablemente* son las once. _____

3. *Me imagino que* el collar vale mucho. _____

4. *Probablemente* hay canela (*cinnamon*) en la torta.

_____

5. *Supongo que* quieres ir a la conferencia. _____

6. *Probablemente* hace calor toda la semana. _____

7. *Me imagino que* Uds. saben lo que pasó. _____

8. *Probablemente* está emocionado. _____

◀ *For more help, see* Future tense, *page 99.*

FF At the office

Mauricio is telling Tere what occurred at the office. To find out what he said, combine each group of elements into a complete sentence in the passive voice, as in the model. Include an agent phrase introduced by por.

MODELO el teléfono/contestar/la recepcionista

___El teléfono fue contestado por la recepcionista.___

1. el documento/escribir/los asesores

_____

2. el presupuesto (*budget*)/aprobar (*approve*)/la junta (*board*) de directores

_____

3. la base de datos/hacer/el programador

_____

4. las páginas web/actualizar (*bring up to date*)/la administradora de web

_____

5. los correos electrónicos/mandar/la administradora asistente

_____

6. las estrategias de mercado/estudiar/el director de marketing

_____

7. las impresoras/reparar/el equipo técnico

_____

8. los productos verdes/vender/los agentes de ventas

_____

◀ *For more help, see* Passive voice, *page 113.*

GG Hotel life

To describe the services and amenities at the Miraflores Hotel, combine each group of elements into a complete sentence, using the se-*construction, as in the models.*

MODELOS   regalar/fruta/para dar la bienvenida (*welcome*)
      Se regala fruta para dar la bienvenida.

      regalar/flores/para dar la bienvenida
      Se regalan flores para dar la bienvenida.

1. subir/el equipaje/sin espera

_____

2. pedir/servicio a cuarto/veinticuatro horas al día

_____

3. servir/champán en el lobby

_____

4. limpiar/las habitaciones/dos veces al día

_____

5. hablar/español/en la recepción

_____

6. poner/a disposición de los clientes/los mejores servicios

_____

7. dejar/chocolates/en la almohada (*pillow*) al atardecer (*in the evening*)

_____

8. proveer/conexión inalámbrica (*wireless*) de alta velocidad a Internet gratuita (*free*)

_____

9. incluir/un desayuno buffet

_____

10. arreglar/excursiones/a lugares turísticos

_____

11. conseguir/taxi/delante del hotel

_____

12. proporcionar/servicios de conserje (*concierge*)

_____

13. encontrar/dos piscinas/exteriores

_____

14. abrir/un restaurante/de fama mundial/este año

_____

◀ *For more help, see* Passive voice, *page 113.*

HH   On the condition that . . .

Some people will do certain things on condition that, provided that, in case, before, unless, or in order that other people do them. To express this, combine each group of elements into a complete sentence, as in the model. Use the future tense in the main clause and the present subjunctive in the subordinate adverbial clause. Use the conjunction in parentheses to link the two clauses.

MODELO   Ud./no cancelar la fiesta : Ángela/no ir (aunque)
  Ud. no cancelará la fiesta aunque Ángela no vaya.

1. yo/salir a la tienda de cómputo : Uds./volver a casa (antes de que)

_____

2. Esteban y Rosa/ver la película : tú/no querer verla (a menos que)

_____

3. nosotros/encargar el libro en Amazon : Manolo/saberlo (sin que)

_____

4. Roberto/escribir el informe hoy : sus jefes/necesitarlo esta semana (en caso de que)

_____

5. tú/comprar una torta de chocolate : nosotros/servir postre esta noche (para que)

   _____

6. Uds./hacer turismo : Fernanda y Felipe/acompañarte (con tal de que)

   _____

7. Estela/retirar dinero del cajero automático (*ATM*) : ella y su familia/poder ir de viaje (a fin de que)

   _____

8. Ud./decirme el secreto : yo/no decírselo a nadie (a condición de que)

   _____

◀ *For more help, see* Subjunctive mood, *pages 117 and 119–120.*

II Winning the lottery

To tell what Andrés and other people would do if they won the lottery, combine each group of elements into a complete sentence, using the conditional tense, as in the model.

MODELO   Andrés/no trabajar más

   Andrés no trabajaría más.

1. yo/ir a vivir a la Isla de Pascua

   _____

2. Verónica y su marido/crear una empresa de artes gráficas

   _____

3. David y yo/poder comprar un Lamborghini

   _____

4. tú/invertir dinero en la Bolsa

   _____

5. Uds./pagar la universidad de sus cinco hijos

   _____

6. Isaac/donar una fuerte cantidad de dinero a algunas instituciones de caridad (*charity*)

   _____

7. Esperanza/usar ropa solamente de alta costura (*haute couture*)

   _____

8. Ud./hacer un viaje a la Luna

   _____

◀ *For more help, see* Conditional tenses, *page 101.*

APPENDIX A

Comparison of interrogative pronouns and interrogative adjectives

Interrogative pronouns
(¿qué? ¿cuál? ¿cuáles? ¿cuánto? ¿cuánta? ¿cuántos? ¿cuántas?)

Basically, *¿qué?* means "what?", *¿cuál?* means "which?" or "which one?", *¿cuáles?* means "which ones?", *¿cuánto?* and *¿cuánta?* mean "how much?", and *¿cuántos?* and *¿cuántas?* mean "how many?"

*¿**Qué** lees?*	**What** are you reading?
*¿**Cuál(es)** de estos libros quieres leer?*	**Which** of these books do you want to read?
*¿**Cuántas** peras quieres? Quiero tres.*	**How many** pears do you want? I want three.

When used with the verb *ser*, *¿qué?* asks for a definition.

*¿**Qué** es un gaucho?*	**What** is a gaucho?
*¿**Qué** es eso? Es un diccionario.*	**What** is that? It's a dictionary.

When used with the verb *ser*, *¿cuál?* asks for information.

*¿**Cuál** es la fecha?*	**What** is the date?
*¿**Cuál** es tu apellido?*	**What** is your last name?

Interrogative adjectives
(¿qué? ¿cuál? ¿cuáles? ¿cuánto? ¿cuánta? ¿cuántos? ¿cuántas?)

¿Qué?, *¿cuál?*, *¿cuáles?*, *¿cuánto?*, *¿cuánta?*, *¿cuántos?*, and *¿cuántas?* may accompany a noun. In this case, they are adjectives, even though they have the same forms as the pronouns.

*¿**Qué** libros lees?*	**What** books are you reading?
*¿**Cuál** libro prefieres?*	**Which** book do you prefer?
*¿**Cuántos** periódicos lees todos los días?*	**How many** newspapers do you read every day?

¿Qué? implies an unlimited choice. *¿Cuáles?* implies a limited one.

*¿**Qué** libros te gustan?*	**What** books (any at all) do you like?
*¿**Cuál** libro prefieres? ¿Éste o ése?*	**Which** book do you prefer? This one or that one?

When used with the verb *ser*, *¿cuál?* asks for information about the noun.

*¿**Cuáles** son los títulos de sus dos libros preferidos?*	**What** are the titles of your two favorite books?

APPENDIX B
Para and *por*

The prepositions *para* and *por* have many uses in Spanish. There are several meanings for each. Here we will concentrate on the most common uses, especially the instances in which they may be translated by the English preposition "for."

1. When *para* means "for," remember the following: **Do Use Para Correctly. Follow these Tips.**

DESTINATION	*Mañana saldré **para Madrid.***
	Tomorrow I will leave **for Madrid**.
USE	*toallita **para la cara***
	face cloth
PURPOSE	*las llantas **para nieve***
	snow tires
COMPARISON	*Hablas español bien **para un norteamericano.***
	You speak Spanish well **for an American**.
FUTURE TIME (DEADLINE)	*Eso es mi trabajo **para mañana.***
	That is my work **for tomorrow**.
TRUTH RESTRICTION (OPINION)	***Para mí,** es importante.*
	For me, it's important.

Para appears in other expressions for which the English equivalents are not always expressed by "for." These expressions should be treated as idioms or separate vocabulary items.

estar para	to be about to; to be on the verge of
para + infinitive	in order to

*Leí el libro dos veces **para comprenderlo** mejor.*	I read the book twice **(in order) to understand it** better.
*Quiero algo **para comer**.*	I want something **to eat**.

Para is used with time and dates.

*Llegaré **para las siete**.*	I will arrive **by 7 o'clock**.

2. When *por* means "for," remember the following: **M**emorizing **F**unny **R**ules **B**ecomes **E**asy **T**oo! *Por* is used when "for" expresses the following.

MOTIVE	*por necesidad* **for** necessity's sake, or **out of** necessity
FAVOR (ON BEHALF OF)	*¿Por quién votó Ud.?* **For whom** did you vote?
REASON	*por eso* **for** that reason; **because of** that
BEHALF	*Lo hago por María.* I'm doing it **for María** (on María's behalf).
EXCHANGE	*Me dio un collar por mi reloj.* He gave me a necklace **(in exchange) for** my watch.
TIME LENGTH	*Juan va a México por tres semanas.* John is going to Mexico **for three weeks**.

Other common uses of *por* are

a. to express "by" with a verb in the passive voice.

El libro fue escrito por Isabel Allende.   The book was written **by** Isabel Allende.

b. to express "by" in the sense of "by means of *or* with."

televisión por cable   cable television

c. to communicate some fixed expressions.

por favor   please

Por is used in a number of expressions in which we use "per" in English.

por año	**per** year
por hora	**per** hour
por ciento	**per**cent

Por, like *para*, can be used before an infinitive, but the meaning is different in Spanish.

estar para	to be **about to**
estar por	to be **inclined to**

Estoy para comenzar a trabajar.	I am **about to** start work.
No estoy por trabajar hoy.	I don't **feel like** working today.

Uses of *ser* and *estar*

Ser and *estar* both mean "to be," but they are used in different situations to convey different impressions.

Ser and *estar* with nouns

Ser is used with nouns to tell from where people come, their relationships, and important groups to which they belong. For things, it describes who owns them and of what material they are made. *Estar* is more temporary. It tells where someone or something is at any given time.

	ser	estar
ORIGIN	**Soy** de Chicago.	
LOCATION		**Estoy** en la biblioteca.
LOCATION OF AN EVENT	El concierto **es** en el parque.	
POSITION		**Está** a la derecha.
GROUPS		
PROFESSION	Don Roberto **es** médico.	
NATIONALITY	**Es** español.	
RELIGION	**Es** católico.	
POLITICS, ETC.	**Es** demócrata.	
RELATIONSHIP	**Es** hermano de Ana.	
POSSESSION	**Es** la casa del señor Gómez.	
MATERIAL	Este vestido **es** de lana.	

No determiner is needed when *ser* is used with a noun of profession, nationality, religion, or politics, etc. However, if the noun is modified, an indefinite article (*un, una*) should be used, just as we use "a/an" in English.

> *Don Roberto **es un buen** médico.*   Don Roberto **is a good** doctor.

Ser and *estar* with adjectives

DESCRIBES ESSENTIAL CHARACTERISTICS (*ser*)	DESCRIBES TEMPORARY CHARACTERISTICS (*estar*)
how people or things are	how people or things are
1. fundamentally	1. at the moment
2. normally	2. temporarily
3. objectively	3. in someone's opinion

Examples of the three uses follow.

Soy *morena.*	I am a brunette. (My natural hair color is dark.)
Estoy *rubia.*	I am blonde. (At the moment, my hair is blonde.)
Pedro **es** *gordo.*	Peter is fat. (He's always been like that.)
Pedro **está** *delgado.*	Peter is thin. (At the moment, he is thin; normally, he isn't.)
Salvador **es** *guapo.*	Salvador is handsome. (He is a good-looking person.)
Salvador **está** *guapo.*	Salvador is handsome. (He is looking particularly handsome today.)
Su casa **es** *vieja.*	Her house is old. (It was built in 1903.)
Su casa no **está** *limpia.*	Her house is not clean. (Normally, it is clean; at the moment, it's dirty.)

Be aware that what is "normal" may change. In the example above, Pedro has always been fat; this is normal for him. If he loses weight, we will say at first, *"Está delgado."* With time, though, we will get used to a thin Pedro. Gradually we will start to say *"Es delgado."* His new shape will have become what we expect to see.

We might think of these distinctions as the difference between definition and description. In the following chart, the *ser* column tells us "who" Roberto is. The *estar* column tells "how" he is.

DEFINITION (*ser*)		DESCRIPTION (*estar*)	
Es Roberto Robles.	He is Roberto Robles.		
Es de Chicago.	He's from Chicago.	*Está en Londres ahora.*	He is in London now.
Es americano.	He's an American.	*Está cansado.*	He's tired.
Es moreno.	He's a brunette.	*Está sucio.*	He's dirty.
Es estudiante.	He's a student.	*Está pobre.*	He's broke.
Es católico.	He's Catholic.		
Es un amigo de Ud.	He's a friend of yours.		

Ser and *estar* with verbs

ser + past participle (to describe an action)

Fue matado por un ladrón.	He was killed by a thief.

estar + past participle (to describe the present state)

La ventana está cerrada.	The window is closed.

estar + present participle (to form the present progressive)

Enrique está preguntándose.	Henry is wondering.

Other Spanish verbs used in expressions for which "to be" is used in English

tener

Tengo *hambre.*	I **am** hungry.
Tiene *18 años.*	He **is** eighteen years old.

hacer

Hace *muchos años que...*	It has **been** many years since . . .
Hace *sol.*	It **is** sunny out.

haber

Hay *un jardín detrás de mi casa.*	There **is** a garden behind my house.

Answer key

Nouns

A 1. la 2. el 3. el 4. el 5. las 6. los 7. los 8. la 9. el 10. la

B 1. una 2. una 3. unas 4. un 5. un 6. unas 7. una 8. un 9. una 10. unos

C 1. unos 2. los 3. La 4. Unos 5. un 6. El 7. Los 8. unas 9. Las 10. unos

Pronouns

A 1. nosotros, nosotras 2. yo 3. él, ella, Ud. 4. vosotros, vosotras 5. ellos, ellas, Uds.
6. él, ella, Ud. 7. yo 8. tú 9. vosotros, vosotras 10. ellos, ellas, Uds. 11. tú
12. nosotros, nosotras

B 1. Los tenemos. 2. La preparan. 3. Las reparo. 4. ¿No lo bebes? 5. No la conocen.
6. Ya las leí. 7. Los llevamos al zoológico. 8. ¿Los compraron Uds.? 9. Lo vendieron.
10. El niño lo rompió.

C 1. Hazlo. 2. No los sirvas. 3. La quiero comer. / Quiero comerla. 4. ¿La debo cerrar? /
¿Debo cerrarla? 5. Pónganlos en la mesa. 6. Ábralas. 7. ¿Las podemos ver? /
¿Podemos verlas? 8. Los estudiantes lo piensan estudiar. / Los estudiantes piensan
estudiarlo. 9. ¿Lo puede Ud. traducir? / ¿Puede Ud. traducirlo? 10. Sácala.

D 1. lo 2. me 3. nos 4. me 5. te

E 1. Se los envían. 2. Se lo lee. 3. Dáselos. 4. Se lo mando. 5. ¿Puedes devolvérmelos?
(¿Me los puedes devolver?) 6. Se lo enseña. 7. Te las voy a mostrar. (Voy a
mostrártelas.) 8. A Ud. se lo voy a vender. (A Ud. voy a vendérselo.) 9. Me lo pongo.
10. Dígamela. 11. Voy a preparártelo. (Te lo voy a preparar.) 12. ¿Se la explicas?

F 1. nosotros 2. ti 3. mí 4. Ud. 5. Uds. 6. mí

G 1. la suya 2. la nuestra 3. los míos 4. las tuyas 5. el suyo 6. el suyo 7. las suyas
8. el suyo 9. la mía 10. los suyos 11. el tuyo (el suyo) 12. la mía

H 1. a 2. b 3. c 4. d 5. a 6. d 7. e 8. b

I 1. Este libro y ése. 2. Estas casas y aquéllas. 3. Estos restaurantes son buenos,
pero aquéllos son mejores. 4. Ese teléfono celular es bueno, pero éste es excelente.
5. Me gustan los coches, pero no me gusta aquél. 6. Estos jardines y ésos tienen flores
hermosas. 7. ¿Quieres aquellos pasteles o éstos? 8. Esa bicicleta es más cara que ésta.

J 1. A quién   2. Qué   3. A quiénes   4. Cuál   5. De qué   6. Con quién   7. En qué
8. Cuántos   9. Quién   10. Qué   11. A quién   12. Cuánto   13. Para quiénes
14. Cuáles

Adjectives

A 1. interesante, interesante, interesantes   2. blanca, blancos, blancas   3. español, española,
españolas   4. andaluza, andaluces, andaluzas   5. buen, buena, buenas   6. joven,
jóvenes, jóvenes   7. fácil, fáciles, fáciles   8. algún, alguna, algunas   9. alemán, alemana,
alemanes   10. gran, gran, grandes

B 1. tercer   2. ninguna   3. mal   4. primera   5. algún   6. gran   7. tercera   8. ningún
9. primer   10. buen

C 1. San   2. Santa   3. Santo   4. Santa   5. San   6. Santa   7. Santo   8. San   9. Santa
10. San

D 1. un pobre hombre   2. una vieja amiga   3. un antiguo general   4. una ciudad antigua
5. una gran mujer   6. un hombre pobre   7. una muchacha grande   8. un vecino viejo

E 1. Jaime es más inteligente que Raúl.   2. Mi hermana es menos aplicada que mi hermano.
3. Es el mejor libro de la biblioteca.   4. El metro es más rápido que el autobús.
5. (Él) es el peor estudiante de la escuela (del colegio).   6. Mi curso es menos interesante
que el curso de ellos (que su curso, que el curso suyo).

F 1. aquellas mujeres   2. este libro   3. esa mesa   4. esos aviones   5. aquel coche (carro)
6. estas sillas   7. esas ventanas   8. aquella puerta   9. esta página   10. aquellos
autobuses   11. esos trenes   12. estos exámenes

G 1. su libro   2. mi escuela (colegio)   3. su casa   4. nuestra traducción   5. sus jardines
6. tus ideas   7. sus cuadernos   8. mis tareas (deberes)   9. tu composición
10. su historia

Adverbs

A 1. fácilmente   2. nerviosamente   3. maravillosamente   4. bien   5. lentamente
6. claramente   7. naturalmente   8. cuidadosamente   9. responsablemente
10. ferozmente

B 1. Él no trabaja.   2. Él no trabaja más.   3. Él no trabaja nunca (jamás). (Él nunca (jamás)
trabaja.)   4. Nadie trabaja. (No trabaja nadie.)   5. Ella no aprende nada.   6. No vemos
ni a Paula ni a Carmen.

Prepositions

A 1. a   2. cerca de   3. en   4. delante de   5. debajo de   6. antes de

B 1. de   2. a   3. a   4. X   5. a   6. por   7. a   8. de   9. a   10. X   11. de   12. a

Verbs

A 1. diciendo, dicho   2. yendo, ido   3. viendo, visto   4. muriendo, muerto
5. abriendo, abierto   6. poniendo, puesto   7. sintiendo, sentido
8. durmiendo, dormido   9. escribiendo, escrito   10. rompiendo, roto
11. haciendo, hecho   12. volviendo, vuelto

B 1. caminan   2. aprendo   3. Entiendes   4. piensan   5. siento   6. muestras   7. juegan
8. pide   9. repite   10. permitimos   11. comemos   12. sigo   13. hago   14. traigo
15. estoy

C 1. está trabajando   2. estoy volviendo   3. estás escribiendo   4. está caminando
5. estamos pidiendo   6. están durmiendo   7. estoy oyendo   8. estás mintiendo

D 1. Hablaba con su novia.   2. Terminábamos nuestro trabajo.   3. Ella hacía un café.
4. Esperaba a mis amigos.   5. El niño dormía.   6. Estábamos preocupados.
7. Vendías tu casa.   8. Ella trabajaba en esta oficina.   9. Estudiábamos nuestras
lecciones.   10. Seguían por esta calle.   11. Iban al centro.   12. Veía películas en la tele.
13. Escribías una carta.   14. Ud. leía mucho.   15. Salía.   16. Ella estaba en el centro.
17. Era inteligente.   18. Nunca perdías nada.

E 1. estaban comiendo   2. estabas viendo   3. estábamos siendo   4. yo estaba hablando
5. estábamos saliendo   6. estaban regresando   7. ella estaba llegando   8. estabas
viviendo

F 1. compramos   2. Prendiste   3. busqué   4. tuve   5. se sintió   6. durmió   7. Escribiste
8. empecé   9. puso   10. hizo   11. dijeron   12. tradujo   13. vinieron   14. fue
15. supiste   16. quise   17. di   18. pagué   19. comimos   20. dieron   21. estuvo
22. caminaron   23. Fuiste   24. pudimos

G 1. No sé si saldrán.   2. No sé si podrá(s).   3. No sé si perderá.   4. No sé si lo haré.
5. No sé si lo sabremos.   6. No sé si lo diré.   7. No sé si abriré la puerta.   8. No sé si
pondremos la mesa.   9. No sé si habrá una reunión.   10. No sé si querrá(s).

H 1. tendrían   2. pondría   3. echaríamos   4. harían   5. escribirían   6. saldrías
7. cabría   8. diría   9. venderíamos   10. querrías   11. habría   12. daría

I 1. Ya he abierto las ventanas.   2. Ya han puesto la mesa.   3. Ya hemos hecho ejercicio.
4. Ya ha llamado.   5. Ya he pedido una pizza.   6. Ya han (hemos) visto la película.
7. Ya han vuelto.   8. Ya hemos escrito el mensaje.

J 1. Ya había salido.   2. Ya había hecho el té.   3. Ya habían jugado.   4. Ya habían vuelto.
5. Ya habíamos hablado.   6. Ya había telefoneado.   7. Ya lo habían visto.
8. Ya habíamos comido.

K 1. ¿Cómo lo habrán sabido?   2. ¿Cómo habré ganado?   3. ¿Cómo habrán llegado?
4. ¿Cómo habremos sacado el premio?   5. ¿Cómo habrás conseguido el trabajo?
6. ¿Cómo habrá reparado el juguete?

L 1. La pelota es tirada por los niños.   2. El mensaje fue escrito por Pablo.   3. El informe
ha sido estudiado por los expertos.   4. Esta cantante es admirada por (de) todos.
5. Los criminales fueron arrestados por la policía.   6. La cena ha sido hecha por mi
abuela.   7. Un nuevo estadio será construido por la ciudad.   8. Un comité será
organizado por el director.

M 1. Dámelo. / No me lo des.   2. Escríbele. / No le escribas.   3. Sal. / No salgas.
4. Dínoslo. / No nos lo digas.   5. Hazlo. / No lo hagas.   6. Véndesela. / No se la vendas.
7. Ponlo. / No lo pongas.

N   1. Dígamelo. / No me lo diga.   2. Ábralas. / No las abra.   3. Óigala. / No la oiga.
       4. Véalos. / No los vea.   5. Hágalo. / No lo haga.   6. Apréndalos. / No los aprenda.
       7. Conózcalo. / No lo conozca.

O   1. pueda   2. entienda   3. quieren   4. sepas   5. escoja   6. vayan   7. vuelve   8. haga
       9. conozcamos   10. sigas   11. vean   12. estén   13. vengan   14. dé   15. pidamos

P   1. hicieran   2. supicra   3. prestaras   4. fuera   5. pasaran   6. fuera   7. recogieran
       8. dijera   9. tradujera   10. hablaras   11. diera   12. volviera

Q   1. hubiéramos sabido, habríamos venido   2. habría ayudado, hubieras pedido
       3. se lo habría dicho, hubiera estado   4. lo habría hecho, me hubiera dicho
       5. hubieras puesto, habrías sacado   6. hubieran estudiado, habrían salido
       7. hubiera estado, habría podido   8. habrías comprendido, te hubieras esforzado

Using your Spanish

A   1. Ya lo preparé.   2. Ya los saqué.   3. Ya las arreglamos.   4. Ya la pusimos.
       5. Ya los hice.   6. Ya la serví.   7. Ya las abrimos.   8. Ya lo corté.

B   1. David comienza a tomar un curso de chino en línea.   2. Claudia y Leonardo quieren
       recorrer Europa.   3. Yo pienso leer todas las obras de Shakespeare.   4. Viviana va a ser
       voluntaria en un hospital de niños.   5. Tú y yo tratamos de encontrar trabajo en una
       empresa multinacional.   6. Sofía sueña con ser actriz en Hollywood.   7. Tú esperas
       perfeccionar tu español.   8. Uds. prefieren relajarse en la playa.   9. Timoteo se interesa
       en participar en una excavación arqueológica.

C   1. Estaba nublado cuando ellos llegaron al aeropuerto.   2. Llovía cuando el avión
       despegó.   3. Estaba despejado cuando el avión aterrizó.   4. Hacía buen tiempo cuando
       Sara y Samuel se registraron en el hotel.   5. Hacía mucho calor en la habitación cuando
       Samuel prendió el aire acondicionado.   6. Lloviznaba cuando Samuel y Sara comenzaron
       a hacer turismo.   7. Había truenos y relámpagos cuando Sara y Samuel entraron en
       el teatro.

D   1. Eran las ocho cuando tú te limpiaste los dientes.   2. Eran las diez y media cuando
       sus hermanas se vistieron.   3. Eran las once cuando Teresa y yo nos pintamos los labios.
       4. Era la una en punto cuando Fernando se duchó.   5. Eran las tres y cuarto cuando
       yo me sequé el pelo.   6. Eran las cinco cuando Arturo y Mariano se afeitaron.
       7. Eran las seis y media cuando su hermano se puso los zapatos.   8. Era medianoche
       cuando sus papás se acostaron.

E   1. ¿Con quién están Uds.?   2. ¿Dónde está el restaurante mexicano?   3. ¿Qué hora es?
       4. ¿Cómo están Camilo y Carmen?   5. ¿De qué es el reloj?   6. ¿Para quién es el iPod?
       7. ¿Cómo son los nuevos programadores?   8. ¿De qué origen es la familia de Isabel?
       9. ¿Cómo estás?   10. ¿Dónde están tus papás?   11. ¿Dónde es la reunión?

F   1. Sí, mándaselas.   2. Sí, préstasela.   3. Sí, entrégaselos.   4. Sí, tráeselos.   5. Sí, dáselo.
       6. Sí, pídeselo.   7. Sí, sírveselas.   8. Sí, regálasela.

G   1. Bailaron elegantemente.   2. Se expresó amablemente.   3. Tocó el piano artísticamente.
       4. Presentaron su regalo generosamente.   5. Cantó hermosamente.   6. Sirvieron la
       comida lujosamente.   7. Reaccionó felizmente.

H   1. No la encuentro. / Mi amor, búscala. La encontrarás.   2. No lo encuentro. / Mi amor, búscalo. Lo encontrarás.   3. No las encuentro. / Mi amor, búscalas. Las encontrarás. 4. No los encuentro. / Mi amor, búscalos. Los encontrarás.   5. No lo encuentro. / Mi amor, búscalo. Lo encontrarás.   6. No los encuentro. / Mi amor, búscalos. Los encontrarás.   7. No lo encuentro. / Mi amor, búscalo. Lo encontrarás. 8. No los encuentro. / Mi amor, búscalos. Los encontrarás.   9. No lo encuentro. / Mi amor, búscalo. Lo encontrarás.   10. No las encuentro. / Mi amor, búscalas. Las encontrarás.

I   1. No, no es inglesa. Es escocesa.   2. No, no son chilenos. Son costarricenses. 3. No, no es italiano. Es francés.   4. No, no son españoles. Son puertorriqueños. 5. No, no es brasileño. Es portugués.   6. No, no es israelí. Es estadounidense (norteamericano).   7. No, no son canadienses. Son indios (hindúes).   8. No, no son chinas. Son japonesas.   9. No, no soy ruso. Soy alemán.   10. No, no somos colombianos. Somos venezolanos.

J   1. Sofía es más encantadora que Mateo. / ¡Qué va! Mateo es tan encantador como Sofía. 2. Las películas son más divertidas que las obras de teatro. / ¡Qué va! Las obras de teatro son tan divertidas como las películas.   3. La señorita Rivera es más cortés que el señor Peña. / ¡Qué va! El señor Peña es tan cortés como la señorita Rivera.   4. La tienda de ropa es más elegante que la tienda por departamentos. / ¡Qué va! La tienda por departamentos es tan elegante como la tienda de ropa.   5. Estos novelistas son más célebres que esos poetas. / ¡Qué va! Esos poetas son tan célebres como estos novelistas. 6. Pedro es más simpático que Carlota. / ¡Qué va! Carlota es tan simpática como Pedro. 7. Los ingenieros son más trabajadores que los arquitectos. / ¡Qué va! Los arquitectos son tan trabajadores como los ingenieros.   8. Las tortas son más dulces que los pasteles. / ¡Qué va! Los pasteles son tan dulces como las tortas.   9. Aquel condominio es más caro que esta casa. / ¡Qué va! Esta casa es tan cara como aquel condominio.   10. Benjamín y Raquel son más talentosos que Rebeca y Aurora. / ¡Qué va! Rebeca y Aurora son tan talentosas como Benjamín y Raquel.

K   1. La   2. el   3. la   4. X   5. un   6. una   7. el   8. una   9. las   10. del (de + el) 11. Los   12. los   13. la   14. X   15. una

L   1. Mario y Benita, reciclen los periódicos. / Ya los hemos reciclado.   2. Clara y Carmen, pongan la mesa. / Ya la hemos puesto.   3. Antonio y Arón, corten el césped. / Ya lo hemos cortado.   4. Maite y Eva, hagan el almuerzo. / Ya lo hemos hecho. 5. Andrés y Araceli, saquen la basura. / Ya la hemos sacado.   6. Victoria y Javier, corran los muebles. / Ya los hemos corrido.   7. Lupe y Felipe, paseen al perro. / Ya lo hemos paseado.   8. Alfonso y Luis, cuelguen los cuadros. / Ya los hemos colgado.

M   1. Alberto está navegando en la Red.   2. Tú estás enviando e-mails.   3. Mi hermano está oyendo música.   4. Leonor está lavándose el pelo.   5. Timoteo está tomando un café en un cibercafé.   6. Mis primas están leyendo unas novelas policíacas.   7. Uds. están viendo las noticias.   8. Gerardo está vistiéndose para salir con su novia.

N   1. ¿Estos abrigos son de Mateo y Gabriela? / No, no son suyos.   2. ¿Esta bolsa es de Juana? / No, no es suya.   3. ¿Estas pulseras son de las hermanas Castillo? / No, no son suyas.   4. ¿Este gorro es de Moisés? / No, no es suyo.   5. ¿Estos pendientes son de Sandra? / No, no son suyos.   6. ¿Estos guantes son del señor Soto? / No, no son suyos.   7. ¿Esta sortija es de tu amiga? / No, no es suya.   8. ¿Estas gafas de sol son de María Rosa? / No, no son suyas.   9. ¿Este paraguas es del profesor Sánchez? / No, no es suyo.   10. ¿Este billetero es de tu padre? / No, no es suyo.   11. ¿Estos suéteres son de los gemelos? / No, no son suyos.

O   1. a. Yo creo que Manolo y Celeste se gradúan en junio.   b. Es bueno que Manolo y Celeste se gradúen en junio.   c. Sabemos que Manolo y Celeste se gradúan en junio. 2. a. Es cierto que Esteban viene a vernos el sábado.   b. Prefiero que Esteban venga a vernos el sábado.   c. Dudamos que Esteban venga a vernos el sábado. 3. a. Todos quieren que Uds. tengan mucho éxito con su empresa.   b. Me alegro de que Uds. tengan mucho éxito con su empresa.   c. Ojalá que Uds. tengan mucho éxito con su empresa.   4. a. Sus papás insisten en que Nora y Osvaldo vayan a casarse en enero. b. Nos parece que Nora y Osvaldo van a casarse en enero.   c. Todos están contentísimos que Nora y Osvaldo vayan a casarse en enero.   5. a. Es verdad que hay problemas con la base de datos.   b. Niegan que haya problemas con la base de datos.   c. Nos sorprende que haya problemas con la base de datos.   6. a. Sienten que llueva el día de la excursión. b. Se ve que llueve el día de la excursión.   c. Temen que llueva el día de la excursión. 7. a. Es necesario que Adriana sea atenta y responsable.   b. Exigimos que Adriana sea atenta y responsable.   c. No es verdad que Adriana sea atenta y responsable.

P   1. Señorita, ¿tendremos que llegar a las ocho en punto? / Sí, Débora, insisto en que lleguen a las ocho en punto.   2. Señorita, ¿tendremos que comprar siete libros de texto? / Sí, Maximiliano, quiero que compren siete libros de texto.   3. Señorita, ¿tendremos que hacer la tarea todos los días? / Sí, Carmencita, les exijo que hagan la tarea todos los días. 4. Señorita, ¿tendremos que aprender todas las fechas de memoria? / Sí, Miguelito, es importante que aprendan todas las fechas de memoria.   5. Señorita, ¿tendremos que leer varios capítulos todos los días? / Sí, Pepe, espero que lean varios capítulos todos los días.   6. Señorita, ¿tendremos que traer la calculadora de bolsillo? / Sí, Inés, necesito que traigan la calculadora de bolsillo.   7. Señorita, ¿tendremos que escribir composiciones? / Sí, Paquito, es bueno que escriban composiciones.

Q   1. Roberto y Leonardo se hablan por celular.   2. Marisol y César se entienden bien. 3. Ud. y yo nos conocemos bien.   4. Marta y Moisés se quieren.   5. Diana y Rosa se ayudan mucho.   6. Tú y yo nos tuteamos.   7. Paco y María se compran regalos. 8. Octavio y yo nos escribimos muchos correos electrónicos.

R   1. Nosotros debemos enseñárselo.   2. Tú puedes servírselos.   3. Hay que leérselo. 4. Yo pienso entregárselo.   5. Uds. deben contársela.   6. Nosotros podemos prestártelas.   7. Ud. va a explicársela.   8. Ellos piensan traértelos.

S   1. ¿Adónde fuiste ayer?   2. ¿Con quién saliste?   3. ¿A qué hora se encontraron? 4. ¿Qué tomaron?   5. ¿Qué pidieron de postre?   6. ¿De qué hablaron?   7. ¿Por qué no cenaron juntos?   8. ¿Cuándo quedaron en verse?

T   1. Sí, pero me gusta más ésta.   2. Sí, pero me gustan más aquéllos.   3. Sí, pero me gustan más ésos.   4. Sí, pero me gusta más ése.   5. Sí, pero me gustan más éstos.   6. Sí, pero me gusta más aquélla.   7. Sí, pero me gustan más ésas.   8. Sí, pero me gusta más éste.

U   1. Me gusta la música clásica.   2. Les gusta el fútbol.   3. Te gustan los animales. 4. Les gusta el cine inglés.   5. Nos gustan las ciencias naturales.   6. Le gusta la comida italiana.   7. Le gustan los deportes.   8. Le gustan los bombones artesanos.

V   1. trabajara, viviría   2. se mudarían, encontraran   3. tuvieras, serías 4. asistiríamos, pudiéramos   5. ganaran, podrían   6. iríamos, hiciera 7. fuera, vería   8. hubiera, querría   9. haría, pidieran   10. saldríamos, vinieras 11. se pondrían, dieras   12. estuviéramos, estaríamos

W 1. a. Compraría café en el supermercado. b. Tomaría un café en Starbucks camino a la oficina. 2. a. Llamarían al técnico. b. La repararían ellos mismos. 3. a. Se acostaría al llegar a la casa. b. Saldría a divertirse con sus amigos. 4. a. Yo le diría la verdad. b. Yo le mentiría también. 5. a. Romperíamos con ella. b. Trataríamos de cambiarla. 6. a. Invertirían el dinero. b. Donarían el dinero a instituciones caritativas. 7. a. Le prepararía una sopa de pollo. b. Le tomaría la temperatura. 8. a. Yo serviría la comida pidiendo disculpas. b. Yo sacaría a los invitados a cenar en un restaurante.

X 1. Jorge —Sí, vamos a hacer una fiesta. / Teresa —No, no hagamos una fiesta. 2. María Elena —Sí, vamos a salir a una discoteca. / Cristóbal —No, no salgamos a una discoteca. 3. Flor —Sí, vamos a navegar en la Red. / Alicia —No, no naveguemos en la Red. 4. Diego —Sí, vamos a jugar al béisbol. / Paco —No, no juguemos al béisbol. 5. Diana —Sí, vamos a comer una pizza. / Tomás —No, no comamos una pizza. 6. Carmen —Sí, vamos a ver una película. / Rafa —No, no veamos una película. 7. Lucero —Sí, vamos a un concierto. / Graciela —No, no vayamos a un concierto. 8. Verónica —Sí, vamos a oír música. / Claudio —No, no oigamos música.

Y 1. Buscamos un director ejecutivo que defina estrategia para la empresa. 2. Queremos programadores que conozcan los lenguajes y sistemas a fondo. 3. Necesito asesores que encuentren soluciones a los problemas de sus clientes. 4. Quieren un especialista en marketing que sepa analizar los productos desde el punto de vista del consumidor. 5. Buscan un director de finanzas que dirija eficazmente las operaciones financieras de la empresa. 6. Necesitamos vendedores que puedan viajar a menudo. 7. Busco un diseñador que cree sitios web llamativos. 8. Quiero un abogado que tenga profundos conocimientos del derecho comercial.

Z 1. Si no hubiéramos ido a la playa, no lo habríamos pasado mal. 2. Si el hotel no hubiera estado sucio, habríamos estado a gusto. 3. Si los restaurantes no hubieran sido malos, Uds. no se habrían enfermado. 4. Si no hubiera llovido todos los días, habríamos nadado. 5. Si el cine no hubiera estado cerrado, habríamos visto una película. 6. Si me hubiera echado repelente contra los insectos, los mosquitos no me habrían picado. 7. Si nuestros amigos nos hubieran acompañado, nos habríamos divertido. 8. Si no nos hubiéramos quedado en la playa dos semanas, no nos habríamos aburrido.

AA 1. a. No creemos que Gonzalo y Érica hayan regresado de su luna de miel. b. Me parece que Gonzalo y Érica han regresado de su luna de miel. 2. a. Piensan que le has dicho lo que pasó. b. Es mejor que le hayas dicho lo que pasó. 3. a. Sienten que el perro de Elián haya muerto. b. Sabemos que el perro de Elián ha muerto. 4. a. Creen que Santiago se ha puesto gordo. b. Es malo que Santiago se haya puesto gordo. 5. a. Es una lástima que Uds. no se hayan aprovechado de esta oportunidad. b. Es cierto que Uds. no se han aprovechado de esta oportunidad. 6. a. Me sorprende que Mercedes y Javier hayan roto su compromiso. b. Se ve que Mercedes y Javier han roto su compromiso. 7. a. Es bueno que Joaquín haya invertido dinero en la Bolsa. b. Dudo que Joaquín haya invertido dinero en la Bolsa. 8. a. Es mejor que Ud. no haya oído la mala noticia. b. Esperamos que Ud. no haya oído la mala noticia. 9. a. No es verdad que hayamos hecho una excursión. b. Me alegro de que hayamos hecho una excursión. 10. a. Es dudoso que les hayan devuelto el dinero. b. No es cierto que les hayan devuelto el dinero.

BB 1. No, no hablé con nadie. 2. No, nunca voy a ese centro comercial. 3. No, no hice nada hoy. 4. No, no conocí a Aarón tampoco. 5. No, ya no estudio aeronáutica. 6. No, no buscaba a Valeria por ningún lado. 7. No, no he visto a ninguno de los profesores. 8. No, no fui nunca a Perú. 9. Ni Manolo ni Isabel me llamaron.

CC 1. Hablo del edificio que queda en la calle Castaño.   2. Hablo de los profesores que enseñan historia inglesa.   3. Hablo del libro que leí el mes pasado.   4. Hablo de las tiendas de ropa que tienen diseños de alta costura.   5. Hablo de la marca que es la más conocida del mundo.   6. Hablo de los restaurantes que fueron abiertos por Franco Madero.   7. Hablo de las flores que me compró Ernesto.   8. Hablo del documental que se estrenó en el canal siete anoche.

DD 1. Cuando Mateo y Sofía decidieron ver la película, tú ya la habías visto. 2. Cuando yo llamé a Brígida, ella ya se había acostado.   3. Cuando Andrés y yo llegamos al estadio de béisbol, el partido ya había comenzado.   4. Cuando tú viniste a la oficina, la reunión ya había terminado.   5. Cuando Uds. se sentaron a la mesa, el mesero ya había servido el primer plato.   6. Cuando Luz se levantó, nosotros ya habíamos desayunado.   7. Cuando Ud. encendió su computadora, ellos ya habían apagado la suya.   8. Cuando Javier solicitó el puesto, los jefes ya habían contratado a otro ingeniero.   9. Cuando Juan José dejó la propina, Mauricio ya había pagado la cuenta.   10. Cuando Rebeca y Clara entraron en la estación, su tren ya había partido.

EE 1. Ellas tendrán prisa.   2. Serán las once.   3. El collar valdrá mucho. 4. Habrá canela en la torta.   5. Querrás ir a la conferencia.   6. Hará calor toda la semana.   7. Uds. sabrán lo que pasó.   8. Estará emocionado.

FF 1. El documento fue escrito por los asesores.   2. El presupuesto fue aprobado por la junta de directores.   3. La base de datos fue hecha por el programador.   4. Las páginas web fueron actualizadas por la administradora de web.   5. Los correos electrónicos fueron mandados por la administradora asistente.   6. Las estrategias de mercado fueron estudiadas por el director de marketing.   7. Las impresoras fueron reparadas por el equipo técnico.   8. Los productos verdes fueron vendidos por los agentes de ventas.

GG 1. Se sube el equipaje sin espera.   2. Se pide servicio a cuarto veinticuatro horas al día.   3. Se sirve champán en el lobby.   4. Se limpian las habitaciones dos veces al día.   5. Se habla español en la recepción.   6. Se pone a disposición de los clientes los mejores servicios.   7. Se dejan chocolates en la almohada al atardecer.   8. Se provee conexión inalámbrica de alta velocidad a Internet gratuita.   9. Se incluye un desayuno buffet.   10. Se arreglan excursiones a lugares turísticos.   11. Se consigue taxi delante del hotel.   12. Se proporcionan servicios de conserje.   13. Se encuentran dos piscinas exteriores.   14. Se abre un restaurante de fama mundial este año.

HH 1. Yo saldré a la tienda de cómputo antes de que Uds. vuelvan a casa.   2. Esteban y Rosa verán la película a menos que tú no quieras verla.   3. Nosotros encargaremos el libro en Amazon sin que Manolo lo sepa.   4. Roberto escribirá el informe hoy en caso de que sus jefes lo necesiten esta semana.   5. Tú comprarás una torta de chocolate para que nosotros sirvamos postre esta noche.   6. Uds. harán turismo con tal de que Fernanda y Felipe te acompañen.   7. Estela retirará dinero del cajero automático a fin de que ella y su familia puedan ir de viaje.   8. Ud. me dirá el secreto a condición de que yo no se lo diga a nadie.

II 1. Yo iría a vivir a la Isla de Pascua.   2. Verónica y su marido crearían una empresa de artes gráficas.   3. David y yo podríamos comprar un Lamborghini.   4. Tú invertirías dinero en la Bolsa.   5. Uds. pagarían la universidad de sus cinco hijos.   6. Isaac donaría una fuerte cantidad de dinero a algunas instituciones de caridad.   7. Esperanza usaría ropa solamente de alta costura.   8. Ud. haría un viaje a la Luna.